D1527342

BEST CANADIAN ESSAYS
2021

BEST
CANADIAN
ESSAYS

EDITED BY

BRUCE WHITEMAN

BIBLIOASIS

WINDSOR, ONTARIO

Copyright © the contributors, 2021

All rights reserved. No part of this publication may be reproduced or transmitted
in any form or by any means, electronic or mechanical, including photocopying,
recording, or any information storage and retrieval system, without permission
in writing from the publisher or a license from The Canadian Copyright
Licensing Agency (Access Copyright). For an Access Copyright license
visit www.accesscopyright.ca or call toll free to 1-800-893-5777.

FIRST EDITION
ISBN 978-1-77196-437-1 (Trade Paper)
ISBN 978-1-77196-438-8 (eBook)

Edited by Bruce Whiteman
Copyedited by John Sweet
Cover and text designed by Gordon Robertson

Published with the generous assistance of the Canada Council for the Arts,
which last year invested $153 million to bring the arts to Canadians throughout
the country, and the financial support of the Government of Canada. Biblioasis
also acknowledges the support of the Ontario Arts Council (OAC), an agency
of the Government of Ontario, which last year funded 1,709 individual artists
and 1,078 organizations in 204 communities across Ontario, for a total of
$52.1 million, and the contribution of the Government of Ontario through
the Ontario Book Publishing Tax Credit and Ontario Creates.

PRINTED AND BOUND IN CANADA

CONTENTS

INTRODUCTION

Bruce Whiteman

At the beginning of the introduction he wrote for his collection of poems *The Wedge,* published in 1944, William Carlos
Williams said: "The war is the first and only thing in the world
today." As I write these words in the late spring of 2021, there
are wars in many parts of the world continuing today—in
Syria, Afghanistan, Yemen, and Ethiopia, among others—but
it is the pandemic that is really "the first and only thing" on the
minds of people everywhere. It blighted much of the world
during most of 2020, the year covered by this anthology; and
while the virus has begun to fade in some countries, in others
it is still going from bad to worse and threatens to domin-
ate life for another year, perhaps even a good deal longer. *Best
Canadian Essays 2021* begins and ends with pieces about the
pandemic as an acknowledgement of its dominance in global
news and culture alike. The essays of Kevin Patterson and
Hilary Leathem are rooted as much in personal experience
as they are in scientific or medical research, rendering them
ideal bookends for this collection.

But even in the midst of the worst worldwide medical crisis
in a century, and what Sarmishta Subramanian, in the introduction to last year's *Best Canadian Essays,* called a "global

syncope," Canadian writers have continued to write essays on a vast variety of subjects. After all, stay-at-home orders and province-wide lockdowns just feel to most writers like their usual writing life: stuck inside, seated at a desk in front of a computer. It may be somewhat encouraging to remember that the writer usually identified as the first modern essayist, Michel de Montaigne (1533–1592), lived through an outbreak of bubonic plague (albeit a bacterial, not a viral, infection) that killed half the population of Bordeaux, of which he was the mayor at the time. The authorities then were just as hesitant about lockdowns as any Canadian provincial premier; and although there were no vaccines then, visitors did have to show a card demonstrating good health in order to be allowed through the city's *cordon sanitaire*. Montaigne also managed to survive a different kind of outbreak, i.e., the Wars of Religion that dominated France during the last third of the sixteenth century. Essayists, then, like writers generally, have often faced demanding and dangerous circumstances during their writing lives; yet whatever the peril, it represents just one subject among many that they feel compelled to address.

Variety of interests and depth of curiosity have been the characteristic strengths of essayists from the very beginning. Plutarch, whom Montaigne called "the most judicious writer in the world," and who was to Montaigne what Montaigne was to later essay writers, the master of a style and the possessor of an intelligence only to be aspired to, never achieved, wrote on the usual subjects dear to the later ancient philosopher—morality, superstition, Plato (he was in favour of him), Stoicism (he was against it), Epicureanism (he was against that too)—but also about vegetarianism, rhetoric, grief, and many other things, not to mention the famous parallel lives of the Greeks and Romans, which are not really essays so much as potted biographies. What makes Plutarch the patron saint of all subsequent essayists is that his writing is eternally interesting not so much for what it addresses as for the composite portrait it draws of the author. (Guy Davenport once remarked that Plutarch was probably the most civilized man who ever lived.) The same may be said of Montaigne, who was famously more self-conscious about his intentions ("Thus, reader, I am myself the matter of my book"). He called that book *Essais,* from the French verb "essayer"—to attempt, to try—and the word first comes into English in its current meaning as the title of Bacon's *Essayes* in 1597. Montaigne thus characterized a thousand pages of prose on subjects ranging from smells (he thought that his moustache helped to make his sense of smell more acute) to cowardice (he noted that cruel people wept easily) as a kind of first draft of the known world—spitballing, we might say—all seen through the eyes of a very particular person, with no desire to theorize and a curiosity that knew no bounds.

The essay, then, unlike the academic article or the scientific research paper, has usually gloried in its personal element. We remember and value an essayist like Leigh Hunt or William Hazlitt or Ralph Waldo Emerson for many reasons: for their style, their humour, their insights, their companionability. But even when the subjects they address have lost relevance or their passions seem outdated, even embarrassing, we continue to read them because of the personal frame. Glenn Gould's writings, most of which are perhaps too brief to represent full-fledged essays, many of them comprising only record liner notes or book reviews, nevertheless have a perdurable quality in part because of Gould's irrepressible personality. We know his various odd opinions well—Haydn is greater than Mozart, Richard Strauss is the greatest composer of the twentieth century, the live concert is dead and has had its obsequies read, etc.—and yet the work is always larger than its content. That arrow of personal experience in the essayist's quiver has grown increasingly characteristic in recent years, with the growing book-market dominance of personal memoirs. Memoirs of any kind were rare in Canadian literature before the 1960s, and until recently they tended to represent a kind of capstone to a successful life in politics or the arts. Often they were written as retirement projects. These days, the personal account of life in the family or of life governed by various kinds of trauma or of life as part of an underrepresented community is a genre unto itself, and its popularity with readers is reflected also in the essay form. We are captured by such books or essays through their authenticity, their narratives of coming to terms with the hard things that life can throw at humans, or simply their accounts of how people live their lives in a historical or cultural context. Elizabeth Dauphinee's essay in this anthology is far more than a piece about house ownership. It is about seeing one's personal circumstances as part of a much longer and larger historical continuum. Joyce Wayne's essay also comprises a personal story—she was a "red diaper baby"—but it is set within an under-discussed aspect of Canadian social and political history, the Communist Party of Canada.

Of course, there are other personal essays that, while not focusing especially on history in the larger sense, move us by their authenticity in evoking a singular past that is vividly realized and compellingly told. (That memoirs do not necessarily have to be authentic to be compelling we know well from the infamous example of John Glassco's *Memoirs of Montparnasse*. Glassco represented the book as having been written shortly after his time in Paris in the late 1920s, when he was invalided home to Montreal with tuberculosis *and* a venereal infection, but in fact it was written forty years later and is full of fabrications, guile, and score settlings.) More intimate history as recalled and described in rich and memorable language, parodied in the famed and clichéd school assignment "How I Spent My Summer Vacation," evokes our sense of commonality. Neil Besner's and Eva-Lynn Jagoe's essays here are unlikely to find readers with identical experiences—childhood summers spent in the first case fishing in Brazil and in the second in a country house in Catalonia—but the beautiful renderings these writers manage create magic and evoke our own parallel if different childhood memories. Francis Koziar shows us what it is like to be poor in a society that prefers to look the other way. Mark Kingwell comes perhaps the closest here to describing a universal experience—the death of a parent—and he sets his personal story in an almost mythical context to which many readers, and not only men, will respond unreservedly: baseball.

The other essays gathered here respond to various psychological and cultural prompts. Catherine Bush's "Writing the Real" represents a growing body of essays in many spheres, and not just science, concerned with the fact of climate change. Climate change and the pandemic are threatening forces at work in the life and culture of the Inuit beautifully described by Sheila Watt-Cloutier, and even Stephanie Nolen's excellent essay on the growing menace of Ixodidae, the common tick, includes an element of concern about global warming, as increasing temperatures push the range of various parasites farther north. Ian Waddell, who died in the spring of 2021, uses his personal voice to describe an important aspect of Prime Minister Pierre Trudeau's repatriation of the constitution in 1982: the enshrinement of Aboriginal rights in section 35. The poet Rob Winger's essay on technology, poetry, and the present is the most speculative essay in this book. Soraya Roberts explores female superheroes from a feminist cultural perspective. Jenna Butler and Yvonne Blomer, in an unusual two-author piece, converse and narrate their time spent walking and writing poetry in Assisi and Venice.

When I sat down to start reading for and thinking about this collection, I wondered idly where I would be looking for contributions if it were 1921 rather than 2021. (It is worth recalling that the fourth wave of the 1918 influenza epidemic had run its course only the year before, so there is a parallel.) The Canadian literary landscape at that moment looked very different from now. There were just three publishers for

Canadian books: Ryerson Press, McClelland and Stewart, and Macmillan of Canada. Hugh Eayrs had just become the head of Macmillan and published the big book of the year, Louis Hémon's *Maria Chapdelaine* in the translation by W.H. Blake, a lawyer whose other books were mostly about fishing. (Eayrs also published a book of essays in 1921 by the journalist Augustus Bridle, *The Masques of Ottawa,* a series of biographical chronicles of Canadian political figures.) McClelland and Stewart was just beginning to publish Canadian books. That year they brought out titles by Bliss Carman and Duncan Campbell Scott, as well as one of Lucy Maud Montgomery's lesser-known Anne novels, *Rilla of Ingleside.* The three main academic quarterlies still active today—*University of Toronto Quarterly, Queen's Quarterly,* and the *Dalhousie Review*—were already in existence, and the venerable *Canadian Forum* had been founded the year before. After these four venues, the pickings would have been slim. *Maclean's* existed and might have provided the occasional piece, but *Chatelaine,* which much later would play an important role in the feminist movement, was not established until 1928. The *University Magazine,* edited by Sir Andrew Macphail, had come to an end in 1920, and the then new *Canadian Bookman* was mostly a house organ for the Canadian Authors' Association. Literary magazines were nowhere to be found. *Best Canadian Essays 1921* would have been a rather insubstantial book.

The situation today, if far from ideal, is certainly an improvement over that of a century ago. Unlike the United States, Canada lacks an audience large enough to support the kind of journalism that regularly veers into the conventional essay form that can be found in magazines such as the *New Yorker, New Republic,* or *The Nation.* No Canadian newspaper any longer publishes the equivalent of the *New York Times Magazine.* The days of *Weekend* and the *Star Weekly* ended in the 1970s. Yet by contrast to 1921, there are certainly many vital outlets for essays among the monthlies and the quarterlies, and none of these, apart from *Hazlitt,* has yet moved entirely online. The *University of Toronto Quarterly* remains resolutely academic in nature, but both *Queen's Quarterly* and the *Dalhousie Review* are open to essays meant more for the general reader; indeed the former, with its emphasis on the visual, has turned into something completely different from the standard scholarly journal. The *Canadian Forum* ceased publication in the year 2000, but magazines like *The Walrus* and the *Literary Review of Canada* have to some extent supplanted it. Quarterlies that publish work ranging beyond the literary, such as *Canadian Notes & Queries* and *The New Quarterly,* provide receptive homes for essays on a wide range of subjects, as do the more strictly literary magazines such as *Prairie Fire, Brick,* and others. Indeed, the literary magazines are almost universally open to what now gets characterized almost everywhere as creative non-fiction rather than the essay, presumably because of the popularity of personal memoirs, which are normally taken to be true to fact, whatever may be the actual circumstances of the story as told.

What makes for a good essayist? In the opening pages of *Let Us Now Praise Famous Men,* James Agee, speaking for himself and for the photographer Walker Evans, describes the pair, who were sent by *Fortune* magazine (of all publications) to report on the poor sharecroppers in Alabama in the depths of the Depression, as "two angry, futile and bottomless, botched and overcomplicated youthful intelligences in the service of an anger and of a love and of an undiscernible truth." A little further along, he defines the results of their project, which we might now describe as investigative journalism transmogrified into enduring literature (and art), as an "effort to perceive simply the cruel radiance of what is." Allowing for the exception that the writer of essays can be of any age, these descriptions seem to me to go a long way towards characterizing the good essayist's sensibility as well as his or her aspiration. The exceptional essay derives from a passionate feeling, love and anger being perhaps its upper and lower limits, coexisting with a desire for truth, and it aims for the radiance of what is, cruel or not. Passionate feeling and devotion to the truth are only the *sine qua non*s, of course, for the other essential element of a great essay is its expression in language that will "entertain, instruct, stimulate, and educate" its readers, as one scholar of Plutarch's essays has written. None of the essays in this volume sets out to satisfy a pedagogical instinct per se, but they all, in differing ways, do teach us something. They teach us something about the facts of life, such as the dangers of the coronavirus (Leathem) or the growing risk of a high-spirited walk in the woods (Nolen). They teach us something about culture (Roberts) or history (Wayne, Waddell) or social conditions (Koziar). Or they teach us something about the human heart and its aspirations and travails (Kingwell). There is no theory being taught, no results of scientific investigation or statistical research being presented. If it did not sound ridiculously old-fashioned to say so, you could almost say that the half-visible educational part of these essays is a moral one. But it is a moral tincture evoked through poetry. No reader would be likely to remember that Neil Besner's Brazilian mentor, Tardelli, told him that he had a lot to learn. We've all heard that one. But when the writer adds that he remembers that injunction "through a scrim of years that smell of salt water and unfiltered cigarettes," the words come alive and stick in the mind. As for entertainment and stimulation, those seem almost too obvious to require emphasis, although they do not need to be overdone to achieve a great essay and may be even less important than other qualities.

Hilary Leathem's essay in this book provides an *abecedarium* of the coronavirus, including self-evident entries such as "Black Death," "Immunity," and "Quarantine." Some of the other twenty-three letters of the Roman alphabet, however, bring in subjects that, at first glance, seem to have little or nothing to do with the pandemic, "Functionalism" for example, or

"YouTube." Her point is that almost everything can be understood as being organized in subheadings underneath the
highest category that is the virus, "the first and only thing in
the world today," to quote Williams again. And so too the essay
genre, which is capacious, elastic, polyphonic, and unlikely
ever to fade from literary culture. We seem more than likely to
be reading a lot of essays and memoirs about the pandemic in
the coming years, in Canada as elsewhere, just as after World
Wars I and II there was a glut of memoirs and studies arising
from those two cataclysmic events. But writers will continue,
as they always have, to loose their minds and imaginations on
many different subjects. "Our feelings reach out beyond us,"
as Montaigne entitled one of his essays, and they must find
embodiment.

ANATOMY OF A PANDEMIC

Kevin Patterson

To be alive is to be afraid; anxiety is the spirit of this age and, substantially, of all ages. However good things have gotten, at least for those of us in Canada—however low crime and unemployment rates have become, however much war deaths have declined, life expectancy has grown, or HIV, cancer, and age-adjusted heart disease death rates have shrunk—disquiet claws at us. Financiers may advise that what they call the downside risk—the potential for loss in the worst cases—is limited, but at an existential level, we know better. Everything could just go all to hell, no matter how shiny things look. You don't need to be a wigged-out prepper in the woods to suspect it.

Things have always gone all to hell. Over four thousand years ago, climate change came to Mesopotamia, causing drought and a subsequent famine so severe that the world's first empire, Akkad, simply ceased to be. Farmers abandoned their crops and many scribes just stopped writing. For archaeologists, for the next three hundred years: near silence.

This is from *The Curse of Akkad,* written around the time of the silencing:

Those who lay down on the roof, died on the roof; those who lay down in the house were not buried. People were flailing at themselves from hunger. By the Ki-ur, Enlil's great place, dogs were packed together in the silent streets; if two men walked there they would be devoured by them, and if three men walked there they would be devoured by them.

In the third century, the Three Kingdoms war shattered China. The An Lushan Rebellion, five centuries later, shattered it again. Millions died in each of: the Mongol conquests, the nineteenth century's Taiping Rebellion, colonialism in the Americas, the Thirty Years War in Europe—and, of course, the World Wars, which killed, conservatively, over 110 million.

Famine and war routinely bring civilizations low, but though he trots closely beside those two, the horseman who carries off the most has always been pestilence. The Roman Empire's Justinian Plague, which was perhaps history's first known pandemic, is thought to have killed millions in the sixth century and may have further stressed the weakening imperium. Procopius writes contemporaneously that death rates in Constantinople were as high as ten thousand per day:

And many perished through lack of any man to care for them, for they were either overcome by hunger, or threw themselves down from a height. And in those cases where neither coma nor delirium came on, the bubonic swelling became mortified and the sufferer, no longer able to endure the pain, died.

This was humanity's first catastrophic involvement with *Yersinia pestis,* the bacterium that would resurface during the Black Death, killing 30 to 60 percent of the population of medieval Europe. Western Europe's population would not reach what it had been in the 1340s again until the beginning of the sixteenth century. In subsequent centuries, cholera also swept the urbanized world—crowding being a powerful accelerant for non-vector-borne (that is, not insect- or snail-spread) infection. (Paleolithic peoples saw no sustained human-to-human infections; their numbers were too small to keep up chains of transmission.) What John Bunyan called the "captain of all these men of death," tuberculosis, has been with us for at least nine thousand years, since the neolithic period, and has killed more than a billion humans in the last two hundred years alone. It was responsible for 25 percent of all deaths in Europe between the 1600s and the 1800s. It remains the most lethal infection worldwide, killing about 1.5 million people a year, and currently infects one-third of living humans.

Those infections are bacterial, but history's worst pandemic was caused by a virus that swept the world only a long lifetime ago: the misnamed "Spanish" flu of 1918–20 was a strain of H1N1 influenza of unknown origin (any place where pigs and chickens and people live is a candidate). That illness was often complicated by a supervening bacterial pneumonia, for which there were then no antibiotics, and it spread around the world over the course of two years, ultimately killing 20 to 50 million. It killed, on average, 2.5 percent of the people it infected, but certain communities were hit much harder: about 7 percent of Iranians died, a third of Inuit in Labrador, and 20 percent of the Samoan population.

In *The Great Influenza,* historian John M. Barry quotes an American Red Cross worker: "Not one of the neighbors would come in and help. I ... telephoned the woman's sister. She came and tapped on the window, but refused to talk to me until she had gotten a safe distance away." Barry continues: "In Perry County, Kentucky, the Red Cross chapter chairman begged for help, pleaded that there were 'hundreds of cases ... [of] people starving to death not from lack of food but because the well were panic stricken and would not go near the sick.'" Contagion may be a leading cause of death, but the worst thing it ever does is prompt us to recoil from one another—much the greater injury: to our health, to our communities, to whatever it is that stands in the way of this slouching beast.

This January and February, things started looking like they could again go all to hell. (They may yet.) Wuhan, in the province of Hubei, China, is a transportation hub of 11 million built where the Yangtze and Huan Rivers meet. In December, patients began presenting, in steadily increasing numbers, with symptoms and clinical findings suggestive of viral pneumonia. (Pneumonia is an infection of the lungs; it may be caused by viruses, bacteria, or fungi.) Tests for known pathogens capable of causing such an illness came back negative. This raised the question of whether a novel pathogen—an infectious agent not previously known to affect humans—had emerged.

Novel pathogens inspire a particularly pointed sort of anxiety among doctors. Many familiar pathogens are lethal on a broad scale—influenza caused over thirty-four thousand deaths in the US in 2018/19, for instance—but their behaviour is known and tends to be consistent. Seasonal influenza, for example, is active in the northern hemisphere beginning in November; its spread slows dramatically by late March. It is monitored carefully and understood well enough that vaccines may be prepared that are usually effective at reducing disease incidence and severity. We know how to contain this virus, we know which patients will be the most vulnerable to it, and we know, within an order of magnitude, how many will die. The ceiling on that number matters. While the best-case scenario for influenza each year includes many deaths, we also have an idea of what the worst-case scenario is. The downside risk is not infinite.

With novel pathogens, this is not true. The worst-case scenario is undefined. Novel pathogens are not inevitably virulent or necessarily prone to become epidemic, but some of them do prove to be catastrophic—and doctors don't know, when one emerges, what course it's going to take.

The number of ill in Wuhan grew quickly, as did the number of medical researchers paying attention. On December 31, China notified the World Health Organization (WHO) that it was seeing an outbreak of pneumonia due to an unknown agent. By January 7, Chinese virologists had sequenced the genetic structure of this new virus—which has been dubbed SARS-CoV-2 (the illness that it causes is called COVID-19)—posting it online so that researchers around the world could access it. A few days later, an apparent connection to the Huanan Wholesale Seafood Market, in Wuhan, was reported to the WHO, and the market was quickly ordered to close. On March 11, following growing transmission in countries around the world, the WHO declared COVID-19 a pandemic, which it defines as "the worldwide spread of a new disease."

The virus was found to be part of the family of Coronaviridae, or coronaviruses: a large group of viruses that are so named because, when examined with an electron microscope, they appear studded with projections that suggest a crown. Benign instances of coronaviruses cause up to a third of common colds. A more alarming example is the SARS virus, which leapt from an unknown agent (likely bats) to civet cats and caused a multinational outbreak, killing about 10 percent of the eight thousand people it infected, and which hit Toronto, where forty-four people died of the illness. Another coronavirus leapt from camels to humans in 2012 or earlier and causes a type of pneumonia called MERS, or Middle Eastern Respiratory Syndrome, which persists in Saudi Arabia. These new coronaviruses are zoonotic: they originated in animal populations and were then transmitted to humans. Researchers concluded early on that SARS-CoV-2's leap to humans had occurred quite recently, likely sometime last November.

The story of this pandemic is, in many ways, a story about speed. HIV circulated among humans for about six decades before it was noticed. The quickness with which science has identified this new infection and defined the genetic nature of the virus causing it is unprecedented, but this is matched by the virus itself: the rapidity with which it was observed to leap to humans and the rate at which it was seen to disseminate among us has almost no parallel in modern medicine.

Everything about this story is fast: the science, the virus, and the almost instantaneous popular fascination with and fear of unfolding events—spread by social media but also by traditional journalism and a public sensitized by Ebola and 2009 H1N1. The spirit of our age anticipates disaster when once it anticipated flying cars. For a time after 9/11, every loud noise was a bomb and every brown man a bomber. The disasters of our time have been mostly human caused (or anthropogenic, as the climatologists put it). Given human obduracy, this is less reassuring than it might be.

The Chinese government's information management around the COVID-19 outbreak worsened our general unease. China has been more forthcoming than it was with the 2003 SARS outbreak, but even so, it has not been broadly transparent. Frustration over this among the citizenry crystallized over the treatment of Li Wenliang, a thirty-four-year-old ophthalmologist in Wuhan who alerted his former medical school classmates to the outbreak, on December 30, over WeChat, the Chinese messaging and social media platform. After being summoned for questioning by police and signing a statement that his warning had "disturbed [the] social order," he was released—only to come down with COVID-19 himself, dying of it on February 7. The indignation and anger on Chinese social media was uncharacteristically plain-spoken.

The early clampdown on information had many repercussions. Echo Xie, a reporter for the *South China Morning Post,* travelled to Wuhan in the first weeks of the outbreak. As recently as late January, she told me, "a lot of people didn't take it seriously. It's been almost twenty days since the Wuhan health authorities first published information about the coronavirus, but some people still haven't heard about it." She went on to describe some of the people she had met:

> A woman surnamed Xu, thirty-one, said her father, her brother-in-law, and a family friend had all developed severe pneumonia and breathing problems. Her father had caught a fever in early January, after a business trip to the southern region of Guangxi. He was treated for a common cold at first, but his condition kept worsening. He went to the hospital on January 12, where he was not formally admitted as the hospital had no beds left; he was instead put in an observation room—one that he shared with eleven other patients with different illnesses, with no partitions separating beds. An X-ray showed his lungs were infected, but at that time, he could still walk. On January 19, when he got another X-ray, three doctors told Xu that her father was in a very serious situation and there was a large area of shadow on his lungs. Still, he was kept in the same room as others, without quarantine facilities.
>
> People were asking for help online when almost every hospital was full and no longer accepting any new patients. Yuan Yuhong, a professor in Wuhan, posted on WeChat: "Parents of my son-in-law were infected by the coronavirus and they were diagnosed, but now no hospital accepts them."

Severe viral pneumonias are a familiar problem to intensive care units all over the world, and the level of resources that must be devoted to the care of such patients is high, often straining existing health care structures even with the comparatively low numbers of such patients that are usual most years. ICU care is expensive, costing more than $1,500 per day, and maintaining surge capacity—the ability to respond to an abrupt increase in caseload—is correspondingly expensive.

And so, little elasticity exists in most Western medical systems, including Canada's.

The H1N1 influenza strain of 2009 (commonly referred to at the time as "swine flu") is perhaps the most recent outbreak in Canada that can give a sense of what COVID-19 would be like if it spread here in earnest. Intensive care units were profoundly taxed with patients who had needs that were similar to those of the most serious COVID-19 cases. Supporting critically ill patients—those in multisystem organ failure—requires ventilator support, dialysis, and one-to-one or sometimes even two-to-one nursing staff. It takes only a few such cases to stretch an ICU and its staff, together with allied disciplines, such as respiratory therapists, to their limits, or past them.

In the intensive care unit where I work as a critical care physician, in Nanaimo, on Vancouver Island, we began seeing such patients in late December 2009; by January, we were consistently over capacity. Nanaimo is a medium-size city of just over 100,000, and the Nanaimo hospital has nine ICU beds—a little fewer than the national average of about 12.9 beds per 100,000 people. In such a setting, even a handful of extra patients requiring high-level care can put unsustainable pressure on the system. And it did. By March, the nurses, who had worked long overtime hours for months, were spent.

Those days had a frenetic quality to them that lingers in the memory of clinicians. Usually, the patients were admitted through the emergency room after several days of fever and coughing—familiar symptoms of influenza, which progresses just as COVID-19 progresses. When pneumonia supervenes, breathlessness is the most common indication that things are going badly. This is a consequence of inflammation in the lungs limiting their ability to transfer oxygen to the blood and to permit the exhalation of carbon dioxide.

With respiratory distress comes confusion and agitation; if that distress becomes severe, there may be a decision to sedate and intubate the patient—to pass a plastic tube into the trachea in order to force oxygen into the lungs and facilitate the removal of CO_2. The tube is connected to a ventilator and the pressures and volumes of oxygen-enriched air are titrated to adequately support lung function without overdistending the lungs—a narrow window with patients so sick. People with severe pneumonia are often laid prone, on their front, in their bed, usually chemically paralyzed and sedated to the point of anaesthesia. Special intravenous catheters will have been placed by this point, leading to the large veins that drain into the heart, to facilitate the administration of powerful medicines to support blood pressure. Dialysis catheters may also be necessary if the kidneys are failing, and that, in turn, will usually be treated with continuous dialysis machines, requiring a dedicated nurse and the help of kidney doctors.

That process of stabilization and the initiation of life support systems will occupy a physician, a respiratory tech, and three or four nurses for one to three hours, when it goes well. Three such admissions would fill a day—in addition to the care required for other patients, with heart attacks and abdominal infections and injuries from car accidents, which do not go away during a pandemic—and still leave our ICU short a dialysis machine.

This is what clinicians know: a few dozen extra cases—each of which may require many weeks of care—in a winter can be overwhelming. It is impossible to even imagine how hundreds or thousands of such cases would be managed.

In retrospect, after 2009 H1N1—as well as after SARS and the other recent near misses, to say nothing of the fifteen-century history of pandemics—the surprising thing is how little was done subsequently to prepare for the next disastrous outbreak. There are not boxes full of spare ventilators in the basements of North American hospitals, ordered in volume once H1N1 subsided. There are not broadly understood and detailed plans for coping with the toll of caregiver infection, for housing and feeding the many new staff the medical and ICU wards would suddenly require; personal protective gear has not been stockpiled in anything like sufficient quantities—indeed, according to Tedros Ghebreyesus, director general of the WHO, worldwide supplies are already under severe strain.

As much as the COVID-19 story is about speed, it is also about fear. Frightened people behave badly; contagion makes them recoil from one another. This serves the purposes of the horseman, distracting from important problems and their solutions and making marginalized people—some of whom seem often to be deemed culpable for epidemics—even more vulnerable. Plagues preferentially consume, whether directly or indirectly, the poor and powerless; it is a taste they have exhibited since Procopius.

As a barometer of fear and social dissolution in pandemics, othering has a long history; contagion has, for centuries, been associated with disparaged minorities. The Black Death certainly did not inaugurate anti-Semitism, but there is evidence that it propelled it to new depths. More than two hundred Jewish communities were wiped out by pogroms justified by the libel that Jews were responsible for the plague in that they had poisoned local wells. There is a terrible account in Jakob von Königshofen's history of Agimet of Geneva, a Jew who was "put to the torture a little" until he confessed to having poisoned wells in Venice, Calabria, and Apulia, among others. This became a narrative that accompanied the plague as it moved throughout western Europe.

A similar othering effort was applied to gay and bisexual men when HIV was first recognized, attributing the HIV pandemic directly to sexual practices and indirectly to drug use (particularly amyl nitrate, or "poppers") that lowered inhibitions—which is to say, to the queer "lifestyle." Bathhouse culture was implicated—as if promiscuity were only the province of gay men—as was intercourse between men.

The new coronavirus, it has been suggested, arose and became epidemic among humans in China because of the Chinese themselves. Chinese dietary customs were singled out early—though any sort of explanation would likely have served. In the first days of the outbreak, a clip from a 2016 travel show of a young Chinese YouTube celebrity eating bat soup in a restaurant on the Pacific island of Palau was widely circulated. (Throughout much of Oceania, bats—the only native mammal species to many of the Pacific Islands—have long been considered a delicacy.) This was presented as evidence of the unnatural behaviour of the Chinese, which was in turn held to be the proximate cause of the epidemic. The response was disgust and contempt and a chorus of self-righteous disdain—just as is intended when malicious stereotypes are circulated in such situations.

Alongside these noxious comments, a competing—and equally racist—account of COVID-19 began circulating. A paper—later retracted—was distributed prior to peer review arguing that SARS-CoV-2 had such "uncanny" genetic commonality with HIV that it was probably bioengineered, presumably by the Chinese, who have a microbiology lab located in the Wuhan Institute of Virology. This fringe theory (the genetic sequences in question aren't just in common with HIV but with many other viruses) was repeatedly espoused by Tom Cotton, a Republican senator from Arkansas. (He later walked back the claim.)

Sinophobia has acted at a more local level as well. During the height of the 2003 SARS outbreak, business at Chinese restaurants in Toronto dropped by 40 to 80 percent. Restaurateurs in Chinatowns across Canada were seeing customers stay away before the epidemic had even arrived. And, in January, parents in a school board just north of Toronto signed a petition demanding that a student who had recently travelled to China not be admitted to school; it now has just over ten thousand signatures. "This has to stop. Stop eating wild animals and then infecting everyone around you. Stop the spread and quarantine yourselves or go back," wrote one signatory.

The measure of a plague is the number of people it infects and how seriously it sickens them. The number of people it's expected to infect multiplied by its mortality rate yields its prospective death toll. And this, naturally, is the question that draws the most attention: How bad is it going to get? How many are going to die? What are the numbers? People seek numbers in times of uncertainty because it feels like they have a solidity about them. A quantified subject is a tamed one, to some extent.

The R0, or the basic reproductive number, is a tool that allows epidemiologists to describe how contagious a pathogen is in a given circumstance. It is the average number of people who will in turn be infected by each new infection. If it is less than 1, the infection dwindles. More than 1, it spreads. Regular seasonal flu has an R0 of about 1.4; pandemic flu between 1.5 and 2, depending on the strain. Some early calculations estimated COVID-19's R0 to be as high as 4, but as with the mortality rate, successive estimations moderated the result, and by mid-February, most experts estimated it at between 2 and 2.5. Which remains high compared with influenza but is hardly unprecedented. Measles, in unvaccinated and crowded populations, can be as high as 18.

Other numbers are needed to understand how fatal a pathogen is. A point made often, early in the course of COVID-19, was that its mortality rate is much lower than that of SARS (10 percent) or MERS (34 percent). Though it is too soon to pin down the mortality rate of COVID-19, current estimates put it at between 1 and 4 percent. (In Wuhan, where the health care system has clearly been profoundly stressed, it is at the higher of that range. Elsewhere, the early numbers, at least, have been lower.) This follows known patterns: as a general rule, there is an inverse relationship between mortality and spread; COVID-19 has infected many more people than SARS or MERS and has a lower fatality rate.

Paradoxically, the lower virulence of SARS-CoV-2 makes it more dangerous. With SARS, people who were infected but not yet symptomatic were mostly not contagious. When they did fall ill, they often felt so unwell so quickly that they took to bed or went to the hospital—where they became very contagious. Many nurses were infected, but community spread was limited.

With SARS-CoV-2, it seems that many quite contagious infected people may feel well initially or indeed throughout their infection. Decreased virulence is bought at the price of increased contagiousness, and even if infected people are a quarter as likely to die, ten times as many people have been infected, and many more infections are yet to occur. The Spanish flu's fatality rate was under 2.5 percent; the WHO believes it killed about 50 million, though some other estimates go as high as 100 million. Seasonal influenza's fatality rate is generally accepted to be about 0.1 percent—though it, too, is lethal, killing tens of thousands of North Americans every year as a consequence of how widespread it becomes every winter.

There are reasons for optimism and reasons for pessimism.

One point that needs more emphasis is that epidemics have diminished in much of the Global North for good reason. There has not been an uncontained and uncontainable epidemic on the scale of 1918 in over a century. This is only partly because of specific antibiotics, antiviral therapy (for viruses like HIV and hepatitis C), and vaccines. A large part of this is due to affluence and, to a qualified and recently diminishing degree, justice. The poor in the rich parts of the world no longer often die of hunger. For a majority, drinking water is cleaner. The crowding and misery of Dickensian London saw tuberculosis become the leading cause of death among adults; over the course of the twentieth century, that death toll fell 90 percent. Streptomycin, the first effective antituberculosis antibiotic, was made available in 1947, but there was a huge drop in infections prior to that due to improvements in quality of life. There had been some redistribution of wealth, and the very poorest were less poor than they had been. Tuberculosis in most of Canada is almost gone. But, in Nunavut, which has Canada's highest poverty rate, the incidence was recently comparable to Somalia's.

Part of this reduction in illness is also due to the sustained efforts of public health workers. Public health measures work. They worked to contain SARS in Toronto in 2003. Identifying and isolating infected and contagious people reduced the R0 to less than 1. The discipline of public health lacks the drama of the Salk polio vaccine or effective antiretroviral therapy, but it has saved countless lives nonetheless. It may be just beginning to work in Wuhan. Within a few weeks of the outbreak, there was a test for the virus. In a few weeks more, there may be a much more rapid and convenient test, perhaps available at the point of care, which would make isolation measures much more effective.

But the reasons for anxiety are compelling too. A vaccine is at least a year away. There is no drug with proven efficacy against the virus. As of this writing, the virus is present in more than a hundred countries. There are nearly 8 billion humans on the planet; the next-largest population of non-domesticated large mammals is the crabeater seal, around Antarctica: 15 million. We live, worldwide, mostly in cities and now in densities that make us profoundly vulnerable. As Michael Specter, writing presciently in the *New Yorker* about pandemics, has pointed out, few of us can completely isolate ourselves—and, in Wuhan, the lockdown cannot continue indefinitely. In other parts of the world, where the central government is less powerful, it could not even be initiated. People need food; people need medicine; people need one another.

Nothing important about us and our success as a species can be understood except by looking at our interdependencies. If many of us could not come to work—because of sickness, because of the need to care for loved ones, or because of mandated social distancing—then the fabric of our society would begin to tear. Transportation networks would fail; airports would cease to operate. Human beings are ambivalent about their interdependence. To need others is to be vulnerable; when we're under threat, vulnerability elicits fear.

Despite our hopes, and despite the unprecedented quarantine, COVID-19 was not contained in Wuhan as SARS, improbably, was contained and extirpated in Toronto and the other cities it broke out in. The Wuhan lockdown did slow the epidemic, however, and relieved the pressure on the city's health care system, which was failing.

Now, the rest of us brace for a version of what the Chinese experienced. We must now contemplate how much we need one another. The instinct to recoil would be the worst possible response because doing so would ensure that the most vulnerable among us are consumed. And, in a pandemic, that injury would not be purely moral or social—though it would be those too. It would feed the contagion, overwhelm the hospitals, and increase the risk to the less vulnerable. Rarely is the argument for mutual devotion so easily made.

It might be that this pandemic will turn out less severe than what is feared; it might be that the winter spike in Wuhan will not be replicated elsewhere. But, even if we contain this virus, there will be another. And this point, that some threats can be faced only collectively, will remain. We have to learn it.

With files from Echo Xie, whose reporting for this article was supported by the Global Reporting Centre.

UPIRNGASAQ (ARCTIC SPRING)

Sheila Watt-Cloutier

I write this from my home in Kuujjuaq, an Inuit community in Nunavik, northern Quebec, Canada. We're located about 1,500 kilometres north of Montreal, on the tidal banks of the Kuujjuaq River, at a point where the northern extent of the treeline meets the Arctic tundra.

The remoteness of Nunavik has not entirely shielded us from the global reach of the current pandemic, and indeed outbreaks—although small in number—of infection have occurred in two of our communities. And so, for the past two months, I have been living in self-isolation, part of this time caring for my seven-year-old grandson, Inuapik. He's an extremely active little boy, always curious and observant. He has kept me on my toes from dawn to dusk.

It is now early June—the beginning of springtime in the Arctic, that brief period between winter and summer when life is miraculously renewed. The snow, apart from patches here and there, will soon vanish from the land. Our delicate plants, such as the purple saxifrage, fireweed, and poppies, suddenly freed from their covering of snow, are quickly greening again. The snow buntings—*qupannuaq*—always the first to arrive, are being followed by flocks of other migratory birds, among them geese, ducks, loons, and terns. The snow-white winter plumage of the ptarmigan—*aqiggiit,* our Arctic grouse—is taking on its summer camouflage. And our favourite fish, the Arctic char—*iqalukpik*—will soon begin their seaward migration from lakes connected to the upper reaches of the river, where they overwintered, to feed and replenish in the rich coastal waters of nearby Ungava Bay.

This is also a time when families look forward with intense joy to escaping community life for a while, heading to their traditional springtime camping spots near the mouth of the river or on the shores of Ungava Bay. Many of these sites have been occupied by the same Inuit families for generations, and being in any one of these places is to sense immediately the depth of history and connection they hold. In this way, year after year, families simultaneously renew their attachment to the land and to our ancestors. It is a time of storytelling, of remembering who we are. Here, our language, Inuktitut—ultimately a language of the land—reclaims its rightful place. And here our children, according to their age and gender, participate fully in traditional daily activities: learning and absorbing all the essential skills, aptitudes, and attitudes required to survive and thrive on the land when their own time to be autonomous comes. In so many ways, the land never fails to invigorate and teach. Family and communal bonds are restored, and our spirits uplifted. We become healthier in mind and body, nourished by the "country food" the land and sea provide. This includes a varied menu of goose and duck, fresh-run Arctic char and trout, and, of course, *nat-siq,* the common seal, a staple food of Inuit coastal dwellers everywhere. This ample diet is inevitably supplemented by seagull, goose, and eider duck eggs, gathered from islets just off the shore. At low tide we dig for shellfish, mostly mussels, or catch sculpins, a small, spiny fish we call *kanajuq,* stranded in rocky pools by the falling tide. Raw, crunchy seaweed, gathered from these same pools, occasionally complements the boiled *kanajuq*.

With the signs of spring all around me, and my dreams of soon being able to get out on the land again, in season to go berry picking with fellow Inuit women, it's perhaps not surprising that my thoughts have turned to the place of nature in Inuit life. In our language we have no word for "nature," despite our deep affinity with the land, which teaches us how to live in harmony with the natural world. The division the Western world likes to make between "man and nature" is both foreign and dangerous in the traditional Inuit view. In Western thinking, humans are set apart from nature; nature is something to strive against, to conquer, to tame, to exploit, or, more benignly, to use for "recreation." By contrast, Inuit place themselves within, not apart from, nature. This "in-ness" is perfectly symbolized in our traditional dwellings of the past: *illuvigait* (snow houses) in winter and *tupiit* (sealskin tents) in summer. What could be more within nature than living comfortably in dwellings made of snow and sealskin!

This is especially true of our relationships with the animals that sustain us: the *puijiit*—sea mammals—seals, whales, and walruses; and the *pisuktiit*, the land animals, in particular caribou and polar bear. No other people have relied so exclusively on animals as my Inuit ancestors.

In one of the world's harshest environments, these Arctic animals provided everything needed to sustain human life. Their flesh supplied all the nutrition required for a healthy diet. From their skins, cut and worked as needed, clothing and shelter were sewn. The blubber of marine mammals fuelled the *qulliit*—our soapstone lamps—providing light and a little warmth for the snow houses in the depths of winter. From bones, ivory, and caribou antler, tools, utensils, and hunting equipment were expertly fashioned. Thread, strong and waterproof, used with the seamstresses' delicate bone and ivory needles, came from the sinews of caribou and beluga whales. The reliance on animals was total. Other than berries and roots, in some places available at the end of the Arctic's brief summer, there was no plant life, no agriculture, to fall back on should the hunt fail.

Our ancient beliefs held that the animals we relied upon had souls, just like ours, which needed to be treated with respect and dignity. In the early 1920s, Avva, an Inuit shaman from Igloolik, whose descendants I know well from my resi-dential schooldays, as well as from the time I lived in Iqaluit, Nunavut, for almost twenty years, famously summed up these beliefs at the very core of our pre-Christian identity:

> All the creatures that we have to kill and eat, all those that we have to strike down and destroy to make clothes for ourselves, have souls, like we have, souls that do not perish with the body, which must therefore be propiti-ated lest they should revenge themselves on us for taking away their bodies.

Founded on respect, our appeasement of the animals we harvested took many forms: for instance, giving a newly killed seal or walrus a mouthful of water, a practice based on the knowledge from a deep understanding of and connec-tion to the animals we hunt that these mammals, having spent all their lives in the sea, craved a drink of fresh water. Taboos associated with particular animals were strictly observed. In this way, care was taken to avoid mingling creatures of the sea with those of the land, and so there were prohibitions against sewing caribou-skin clothing on the sea ice. Nor could the flesh of seal and caribou be boiled in the same pot. I remember my mother reminding me of this even when I would eat both frozen fish and frozen caribou together. Above all, the absolute bond between my ancestors and the animals they hunted (and, by extension, the land, sea, and air) was founded on respect.

Hunters never boasted about their prowess. Abusing animals in any way, or mocking them, or using them for "sport," resulted in serious consequences for society, as did disputes over sharing. In response to maltreatment or insults, animals would withdraw from hunting grounds. Hunters were obliged to kill only animals who "presented" themselves for the taking. This is exactly why, when I lived in the south and made visits home to Kuujjuaq in the early spring, and we hunted *aqiggiit,* my mother would say to me: "Isn't it wonderful that the *aqiggiit* brought themselves to you so that you could take them back with you to eat in Montreal!" My mother always had that deep Inuit understanding of how life gives life.

There's an ancient tale that vividly illustrates the ethical imperative for Inuit of respecting animals when they "present" themselves, a story that explains why walruses disappeared from a place called Allurilik, a large inlet on Ungava Bay, just over two hundred kilometres northeast of my home in Kuujjuaq. It is said that here there was once a hunter out on his *qajaq* (kayak) looking for walruses. Suddenly, a small walrus surfaced in front of him and begged to be taken because it craved a drink of fresh water. Noticing that this little walrus had very small, deformed tusks, the hunter refused, saying: "Go away . . . I don't want you. Your tusks are too small and deformed!" Hearing these words, the walrus was deeply offended and went away. Shortly after that incident, all the other walruses left the area and never came back. It is said that the caribou, after hearing about the insult, also abandoned the land around Allurilik. The lesson here is that all animals presenting, or in my mother's words "bringing" themselves to the hunter, should be understood not as confirmation of death, but affirmation of life.

Indigenous communities and cultures everywhere have been ravaged by contact with the Western world. Introduced diseases, against which they had no resistance, decimated their populations. Christianity—usually the forerunner of coloni-alism—pushed aside Indigenous belief systems, altering the way they viewed the world, and endangering their mutual bonds with nature, with the land, animals, and forests that sustained them.

Europeans first came into contact with my Inuit ances-tors on the south shore of Ungava Bay just over two hundred years ago. From that moment forward, our essential one-ness with the natural world was challenged and would even-tually change forever. Like the start of any infection, at first the symptoms were subtle. In those early days of contact, the Arctic, in the European imagination, offered nothing worth exploiting. Our land was dismissed as a barren wilderness, covered in snow and ice for most of the year, inexplicably inhabited by a few nomadic "heathens." Above all, the Arctic, with its ice-filled summer seas, was seen as a sort of adversary to be heroically conquered in Europe's futile efforts to find a northwest passage to the "riches of the Orient."

Regardless, wherever Europeans "discovered" Indigenous peoples, commerce and Christianity were sure to follow and my Arctic homeland was no exception. In time, the inescap-able reach of the Europeans extended to our shores. We named them "Qallunaat." Men of the Hudson's Bay Company were the first to arrive, setting up, in 1830, a trading post on the east side of the Kuujjuaq River, more or less across from the place where the modern community of Kuujjuaq now stands. Shortly after the turn of the century, an Anglican mission was also established there, joined by a Catholic mission in 1948.

We slowly began to accept these strangers in our land and over time we gained some understanding of their ways. But through coercion, when our own powerful spiritual beliefs, which included shamanism, drum dancing, and throat singing, were forbidden and considered "taboo," our people eventually converted. The traders' goods were an obvious convenience, especially metal items such as needles, knives, kettles, traps, and firearms, joined later by an increasing selection of woven fabrics, sewing materials, and basic foodstuffs, including flour, lard, sugar, and tea. And, of course, tobacco. Although we could not have known it at the time, the seeds of consumerism, profound and dangerous changes to our diet, and new diseases were unobtrusively planted among us. We distanced ourselves from the Qallunaat, and our interactions with them tended to be irregular and infrequent. We continued to live on the land, moving predictably from place to place in harmony with the animals, which had sustained us for countless generations. From time to time, usually travelling by dog team, visits were made to the post to trade furs, or to celebrate Christmas at the mission. Yet despite this distancing, our way of life, our unity with nature, was to change forever. Our traditional perception of time, for example, which had ticked to nature's clock—the rising and setting of the sun, the position of the stars, the cycle of the tides, the succession of the moon months—now needed to make room for the Christian calendar. Suddenly there was a unit of time called a "week"; how very strange the idea must have seemed to my ancestors that one in every seven days was a special day when hunting and all other "work" had to stop! Similarly, the traders' constant need for fur, especially white fox, began to alter our subsistence patterns as we spent increasingly more time on our traplines during winter.

Throughout this initial period, which lasted from the mid-1930s to the late 1950s, of coming to terms with the now permanent presence of traders and missionaries in our lands, our lives remained relatively unchanged. We continued to live in extended family groups, distributed along the coast of Ungava Bay. Our culture, values, and traditions remained strong, as did our language, which easily incorporated new concepts and objects brought from the south. "Sunday," for example, we called *allituqaq*, literally a time when we have to "respect a taboo"—in this case the taboo against hunting on that particular day. And the kettles and pocket knives we bought from the traders were named *tiqtititsigutik* or *uujuliurutik* (that which is used to boil something) and *puuttajuuq* (that which regularly unfolds). So we slowly adapted to the newcomers, integrating their ideas and material things at our own pace. In the beginning we came to view this new relationship with the Qallunaat world as essentially balanced and sustainable. Above all, by continuing our life on the land, usually several days of dog-team travel away from the Qallunaat dwellings, we were able to retain our autonomy over the aspects of our lives that mattered most. This included our bonds with the land (including the sea ice) and its animals; and, most important of all, teaching our children the traditions, philosophies, and skills needed to continue this land-based life.

Looking back on this period we certainly did not think that this way of life would last forever. And indeed, it didn't. In the 1950s and early 1960s the Canadian government suddenly took an interest in "its territories" in the Far North. Focus on the area first came from the construction of the so-called Distant Early Warning Line, a sort of necklace of defence radar stations built by the US military above the Arctic Circle, from Baffin Island, Canada, to Wainwright, Alaska. With advancing technology and increasing explorations by prospectors, mineral exploitation in the Arctic was becoming a real possibility. And there were also tragic reports of inland-dwelling Inuit in Canada's "barren grounds" starving to death. The Canadian government decided it was time to act. Without any meaningful consultation, they instigated a policy to move Inuit from the land into settlements that, in most instances, would be built at sites previously established by the Hudson's Bay Company and the missionaries.

From the start, the government's policy to move us "off the land" was misguided and paternalistic. The idea was to make the "administration" of Canada's Eskimos (as we were then called) easier. We were seen as a problem needing to be fixed. This would be mended by gathering us into settlements, building houses for us, and "educating" our children in English with a "Dick and Jane" curriculum, an education that had nothing to do with what we knew to be the real world. We would partake of the government's assistance programs such as family allowances (which sometimes could be withheld if we didn't send our children to school) and, when needed, social assistance payments and subsidized housing. Along with the provision of health services, these seemingly positive enticements were difficult to resist. Nowadays we recognize these offerings as coercive, though strangely packaged in well-meaning wrappings.

In my case, our family's move into the settlement happened in 1957, earlier than for most Inuit then living in the Canadian Arctic. At the time, we were living at Old Fort Chimo, where I was born, and where the Hudson's Bay Company still ran a trading post. Across the river from us, the US military had built a weather station and landing strip during the Second World War, one of several airstrips on a northern route to Europe, along which the Americans used to ferry aircraft to Britain. After the war the US transferred the site's buildings and airstrip to the Canadian government and in time, under its "ingathering of Inuit" policy, these became the present-day community of Kuujjuaq.

With the move, things happened very quickly. At first, we expected that this new world in which we suddenly found ourselves would be as wise as our own. But it wasn't. It turned out that our new world was deeply dependent on external political and economic concepts and forces utterly at odds with our ways of being. In particular its structures seemed to have nothing to do with the natural world. Almost immediately, we started to give away our power. For a while we thought that if we were patient—as the Inuit hunters necessarily are—that patience would pay off. But we soon lost that sense of control over our lives, especially over the upbringing of our children. They were brought into the classrooms of southern institutional schooling, a concept totally foreign to us, where they were given an "education" that had nothing to do with the knowledge and skills we needed for life on the land. All our traditional character-building teachings went out the window, and our social values began to erode. When we surrender our personal autonomy, we also give away our sense of self-worth, we lose the ability to define ourselves and to navigate our own lives. Being brought into the settlements was the beginning of the end for our traditional way of life. In the settlements we lived in a kind of bubble, separated from the natural world, exchanging our independence for increasing dependency.

In this new, confusing life—which, at least on the surface, seemed to meet all our basic needs—we also lost, above all, our sense of purpose. In our attempts to replace this loss with something else, many of us drifted into addictions and self-destructive behaviours, made worse by unemployment and poverty. This downward trend has played out over several generations in the most horrific ways, seen most tragically in the current levels of suicide among Inuit youth.

I was in my late teens when we experienced our first suicide in Kuujjuaq, a young Inuit woman, though she was not actually from our community. Traditionally suicide, in Inuit society, was rare and affected mostly adults, so this was shocking and incomprehensible to us all. Nowadays it's a tragic fact that our Inuit youth suicide rates are among the highest in the world. I have no doubt whatsoever that this tragedy is rooted in our move from the land, and the subsequent erosion of our culture and values, not to mention the historical traumas of forced relocations, the slaughter of our sled dogs, and abuse in many forms by those with authority. Whatever the underlying causes, these suicides can often be impulsive. In our traditional ways, impulsivity had no place. On the land, to act impulsively was to put yourself and everyone else around you at risk. Even under extreme pressure, decisions had to be weighed carefully. In our upbringing we were taught to develop that sense of holding back, of reflecting and being focused: our very lives depended on us avoiding any urges towards reckless behaviour.

Along with many others of my generation, I was fortunate enough to have spent my formative years deeply steeped in Inuit traditional ways and values that gave us our understanding of the world and our place in it and, importantly, our responsibilities to it. My age group still talks about this—that sense of training and the grounding we got, which have kept us going and made us resilient.

My early years in Kuujjuaq cocooned me in these traditions thanks, primarily, to two incredibly strong women: my mother and my grandmother. I also learned by observing my uncle, a skilled hunter and community leader with a lot of integrity and dignity, as well as my older brothers, who had been taught many skills by my uncle and other men in our community. Beyond these, teachers enough in themselves, were the always gently instructive social interactions I enjoyed with the small community around us. This supportive and caring circle was occasionally enriched by Inuit visitors from other parts of Ungava Bay, coming into Kuujjuaq to trade, travelling by dog team in the winter or canoe in the summer. To this day I can vividly recall their words as I sat, silent and wide-eyed with amazement, listening to them relate their news and stories to my mother and grandmother.

Of course, these occasions were always an opportunity to liberally share in whatever country food we had at hand. Depending on the season, this could be any combination of fish, ptarmigan, seal, and the choice parts of caribou, raw, dry, frozen, or cooked, according to preference. Most often these foods would be enhanced by our traditional condiment, a dipping sauce we called *misiraq*, made from fermented seal oil. Sharing the food our land provides is a deeply held Inuit tradition, indeed an imperative—there's no other word for it.

Wherever we are, this practice is still at the core of our family and community life. In this unspoken ritual, sharing nature's bounty renews, again and again, our bonds with each other and the land that sustains us.

I have an early memory that brought all these strands together, underscoring our essential place within nature that I didn't fully understand at the time. Inuit have many categories of relationships and relationship terms without an exact equivalent in the Western world. Traditionally, personal names given at birth were said to carry souls and they immediately established a wide network of relationships, even mutual responsibilities, often extending beyond the immediate family. Nor were personal names ever gendered. For instance, a baby boy named after, say, his maternal grandmother would be addressed by his own mother as *anaana*—meaning mother—and, in some cases, at least until puberty, would be dressed and even socialized as a girl. Family members would notice with delight how he took on some of his grandmother's personality traits and mannerisms. In this way, his grandmother continued to live through him.

A particularly significant relationship, in terms of linking community and nature, was initiated at birth with the person who cut the umbilical cord, usually a woman. If the baby was a girl, this woman would be known as her *sanajik*; if a boy, she would be his *arnaqutik*. The baby then became the *arnaliak* of her *sanajik*, or the *angusiak* of his *arnaqutik*.

Both my grandmother and mother were known for their midwifery skills, and so they had a good number of *angusiaks* and *arnaliaks*. One of the main obligations of their angusiaks was to present them with their first catch from the hunt—be it fish, seal, ptarmigan, or caribou, a rite of passage, celebrating the very foundations of Inuit society: that is the sacred, interdependent relationship between the animals we hunt and our hunters. When I was a small girl, I saw this ritual played out many times as these budding hunters—my grandmother's *angusiaks*—honoured their obligations to her. One at a time, every other month or so, young men would come by our house to present their catch. In response my grandmother put on an amazing performance. This normally quiet, dignified elderly woman would suddenly turn into an animal-like person, rolling around and making animal noises on the floor. Sometimes she would nibble the young hunter's hand or wrist, acknowledging their power, encouraging him to become a great hunter. I watched this startling performance almost in embarrassment because then, as a child, I didn't fully grasp its deep ceremonial significance, beyond sensing it was a necessary part of our hunting culture.

For their part, the girls and young women who were my grandmother's and mother's *arnaliaks* would be similarly honoured and encouraged when they brought gifts demonstrating their increasing ability in sewing. Proper, well-made skin clothing, warm and watertight as needed, was an absolute necessity for the successful provider. Inevitably my grandmother's ritual would finish with the young men or women we had just celebrated leaving the house confident and reassured, knowing that their work or hunt had been well received, endorsed by the woman who had helped to bring them into this life.

Sadly, this ancient custom is not much practised now. Though from my early years working at the Kuujjuaq nursing station, I assisted at several births and therefore have my own set of *angusiaks* and *arnaliaks*. I do my best to keep up with them, encouraging them over the years as they successfully fulfill their varied roles in life. Some of the young men have brought me their first hunt; the young women, gifts of their picked berries, caught fish, or first pieces of handiwork. My response was not as dramatic as my grandmother's, but it was no less full of delighted gratitude. I was humbled and honoured that they had thought to keep this tradition alive.

Despite the extensive damage done to Inuit society and culture when we moved from the land into the villages, there is, in most of these settlements, an essential core of families instinctively committed to maintaining our traditions. Individual members of these families, even while living within the semi-urban settings, strive to relate to the land and its resources in the same respectful way that sustained us prior to the move. They acquire an intimate knowledge of their local area and the various animal species it supports. The men employ many of the same hunting skills used in former times while the women prepare and soften the skins of seals and caribou for the clothing they make for themselves and their hunters, using techniques, patterns, and stitches handed down by an endless succession of mothers, aunts, and grandmothers. Most importantly, members of these families embody the essential philosophies and understandings of the land and animals that enabled us to thrive over countless generations before we suffered the consequences of European contact. In a real and substantial sense such Inuit keep the vital flame of our culture alive. They are an irreplaceable resource, in both practical and intellectual ways, and they need and deserve every possible means of support.

But beyond the challenges this already vulnerable way of being endures, in the face of the Arctic's rapidly increasing urbanization (and globalization), there is another imminent threat—no less insidious—that, unless checked, will end forever our unique attachment to the land and its life-giving resources: climate change.

Dramatic climate change caused by greenhouse gases has left no feature of our Arctic landscape, seascape, or way of life untouched. Climate change now threatens our very culture, our ability to live off the land and eat our country foods. Nowhere else in the world are ice and snow so essential to transportation and mobility. And yet the snow and ice coverings over which we access our traditional foods are becoming more and more unreliable and therefore unsafe, leaving our hunters more prone than ever to breaking through unexpectedly thin ice or being swept out to sea when the floe-ice platform, on which they are hunting, breaks off from the land-fast ice.

Additionally, climate change is affecting the migration patterns and routes of the animals we rely upon. This means that our hunters have to travel farther, often over unsafe and unfamiliar trails, to access our country food. So, when we can no longer count on our vital, long-established travel routes, and can no longer find the animals where they should be, the matter immediately becomes an issue of safety and security at several levels.

With less traditional food available, many families are forced to shift away from our traditional food to a far less healthy diet shipped from the south, consisting mainly of processed foods crammed with sugar, salt, and carbohydrates. It is no surprise that in Canada our Arctic communities are experiencing rapidly rising rates of diabetes and other food-related illnesses, trends that will only continue as we move away from a country-food diet.

Hand in hand with climate change is the ongoing threat of Arctic resource development targeting our rich mineral and oil deposits. Our anxieties on this front are regularly dismissed by our own governments who see the Arctic as the next super-energy "feeder" for the world. In the greater scheme of things, Inuit concerns over their livelihoods and environment are dismissed as unimportant.

As someone who has led pioneering global work on connecting climate change to human rights, I am convinced that the escalating pressures we now face regarding resource development will deepen the need for all parties to adopt a rights-based approach in the search for solutions to these problems.

Everyone benefits from a frozen Arctic. The future of the Arctic environment, and the Inuit it supports, is inextricably tied to the future of the planet. Our Arctic home is a barometer of the planet's health: If we cannot save the Arctic, can we really hope to save the forests, the rivers, and the farmlands of other regions?

We can also no longer separate the importance and the value of the Arctic from the sustainable growth of economies around the world. In the international arenas, where I have personally been involved, the language of economics and technology is always calling for further delays on climate action. We are constantly reminded that making any significant efforts to tackle greenhouse gas emissions will negatively impact the economy. But I truly believe that we must reframe the terms of the debate regarding the implications of environmental degradation, resource development, and climate change in the Arctic and move beyond relying solely on the language of economics and technology. What is needed is a debate emphasizing human and cultural rights. Focusing only on economics and technology separates the issues from one another as opposed to recognizing the close connections among rights, environmental change, health, economic development, and society. Ultimately, addressing climate change in the language of human rights and building the protection of human rights into our global climate agreements are not just matters of strategy, but moral and ethical imperatives that require the world to take a principled and courageous path to solve this great challenge.

And I strongly believe that we need to reimagine and realign economic values with those of the Indigenous world, the Inuit world, rather than merely replicating what hasn't worked with the values of Western society. And who better than the Inuit themselves, who are natural conservationists, to be out there on the land and ice as paid guardians and sentinels? How deeply affirming that would be for our hunters, whose remarkable traditional knowledge is so undervalued. What better way to reclaim what was taken from us: our pride, our dignity, our resourcefulness, our wisdom. We don't want to just be victims of globalization. We can offer much more to this debate if we could be included on every level. We have lived through states of emergency for decades now and we have attempted to signal to the world the climate crisis looming in front of us. Sadly, many in other parts of the world who are now experiencing these states of emergency, with the loss of their homes and livelihoods to fires, floods, and other unnatural disasters caused by climate change, are finally beginning to see the connections.

So my message to you is: look to, listen to, and support morally, respectfully, openly, and, yes, financially the Inuit world, the Indigenous world, which from a place of deep love for their culture and traditions is fighting for the protection of a sustainable way of life. Not just for themselves, but for all of us. Heed and support those voices and their aspirations. We will help guide you as we navigate through these precarious situations together. Don't be on a mission to save us: this is not what we want or need. But together in equal partnership, with an understanding of our common humanity, we can do this together.

Epilogue

I began writing this piece in my Arctic home in Kuujjuaq. I am still here; still following the recommended social distancing and self-isolation measures brought on by the pandemic, a grim reminder of how interconnected and interdependent we all are. The remoteness of the Arctic no longer sets us apart from the rest of the world. This pandemic has also helped to break open unresolved issues of social injustices and racism: North American and European countries that often tout their great human rights reputations are now being fully exposed for outdated racist policies and attitudes which undermine, and put at great risk, the health of those most vulnerable. Black communities, the American Indian nations, and our own Indigenous populations here in the Arctic show clearly that the economic and health gaps are huge in comparison to the white populations of rich countries. The only difference that sets us in the Arctic apart from our Black and Navaho brothers and sisters with the human losses they have suffered is that to date, as I write this, the geographic distance we live in and the lockdown of flights coming in and out of our regions have thus far protected us. That could easily change overnight if and when there is a resurgence of the virus. History has shown us that many Inuit families were wiped out by past epidemics, so our leaders are extremely committed in their attempts to keep the virus out of our regions.

In many different ways, the pandemic has also given us pause. I have been taking the time to use this pause as a gift to reflect on new possibilities, new perspectives. The world should not, cannot, go back to business as usual without a clearer understanding and consciousness of how we live.

In my life's work, dealing with climate change and the protection of our Inuit way of life, I have often wondered what is going to eventually "give"? What big event will finally wake us up to the realization that the reckless, damaging way in which we do business around the world is unsustainable? In my talks, I often ask: "What will it take to get the health back into our atmosphere so the earth can start to heal?" The earth is a living, breathing entity. If we care for it, it will heal just as our bodies do when we are sick.

I have always sensed the earth would reach its limits soon enough, but I didn't realize it would be in the form of a deadly virus that would virtually halt (at least temporarily) so many of our unsustainable activities. Almost immediately, the air and the waters of the world's industrial cities began to clear. Animals, suddenly relieved from unwelcoming human activity, appeared in some deserted city streets, as if reclaiming their rightful space. Nature is resilient, if only given the chance. Let's pay heed to these lessons. Let's make this a time of seeing that human trauma and planet trauma are one and the same. Let's not wait for another virus, driven by climate change and environmental degradation, to terrify us, too late, into half-hearted action. There is no time for half measures. The values and knowledge of the Indigenous world, the survival of which utterly depends upon living within nature, not apart from nature, hold the answer to many of the global challenges we face today. Indigenous wisdom is the medicine we seek in healing our planet and creating a sustainable world. I truly believe this.

TICK TOCK

Inside the Quest to Track One of Humanity's Tiniest Deadly Predators

Stephanie Nolen

When Katie Clow and her research students arrive in a windowless lab at the Ontario Veterinary College, in Guelph, Ontario, on a drizzly late fall morning, envelopes have piled up on their workbench like a manila snowdrift. They slip on white coats and reach for scissors to start slitting open the padded packets. Each one contains a slip of paper and a small plastic vial or two. The paperwork lists the name of a veterinary clinic somewhere in Canada and the identifying details of someone's pet: a six-year-old golden retriever in Moncton, a four-year-old tabby in Victoria.

Inside each corresponding vial is a tick—or fifty—plucked from the body of that pet and mailed in for research. With her team, Clow, a professor of veterinary medicine with expertise in epidemiology and ecology, opens the vials and tips the rigid bodies of the arachnids into a petri dish. Unless they're not dead: after a week or two in the custody of Canada Post, they sometimes emerge and start scurrying across the bench. When an alive one tumbles out in front of research assistant Kiera Murison, she snatches a pair of tweezers to pluck it up and deposits it into a vial of ethanol, with a whispered apology, swirling it around to bring a prompt demise.

When the ticks are all definitely dead, they are stored in the fridge until Clow, an ebullient thirty-two-year-old whose students call her the Tick Queen, has time to sit down with a box of them. She identifies the ticks quickly, by species and by gender, based partly on the appearance of their hard outer shell, called a scutum, and sometimes by the shape of their protruding mouthparts. Most of the ticks mailed to her Canadian Pet Tick Survey are American dog ticks, *Dermacentor variabilis,* or blacklegged ticks (also called deer ticks), *Ixodes scapularis:* those are the two types you are most likely to find on your pet or your tent or your toddler this summer.

Once identified, the ticks go under the knife: with a scalpel blade, Murison slices them to bits. Ticks that were found and removed before they had time for a long feed are smaller than a watermelon seed and nearly as crunchy: they resist the scalpel. But the engorged ticks, the ones that had a hearty blood meal, can be swollen up like a stewed cranberry. Cutting them is more like carving a soggy M&M. "You definitely hear the outer shell breaking," says Murison, hacking away at a rigid American dog tick so vigorously that her blond ponytail swings back and forth. When the engorged ticks are dissected, they give off a loamy smell from the coagulated blood that has ballooned them to as much as ten times their original size. Clow and her team marinate the chopped ticks in chemical reagents then run them through a process that extracts the DNA in the bug hash. There are two main types of genetic material they are looking for in blacklegged ticks: that of *Borrelia burgdorferi,* the bacteria that causes Lyme disease, and *Anaplasma phagocytophilum,* the cause of anaplasmosis, which brings fever and vomiting and, in rare cases, can cause respiratory and organ failure. Clow finds *B. burgdorferi* in about 25 percent of samples; *A. phagocytophilum* is much more rare, found in just 1 to 2 percent.

Murison shoves aside a heap of envelopes and shakes her head at the pile. "We're not supposed to be getting this many in October," she says. There are ticks in all seasons now. Lyme rates are surging because the ticks that spread it—*I. scapularis,* predominantly—are rapidly expanding their range. Climate change has made much of the most populated part of Canada an ideal habitat for many species of ticks; *I. scapularis,* which spreads Lyme, in particular, is rapidly expanding its range. In the early 1970s, there was just one known colony of blacklegged ticks in Canada, at Long Point, on the north shore of Lake Erie. By the 2000s, the tick was being found all over southern Ontario, Quebec, Manitoba, and the Atlantic provinces. Today, they're marching steadily west from Manitoba on their eight tiny legs.

I. scapularis is no bigger than a poppy seed when it does most of its damage, but this particular tick is emerging as an outsize threat. "Their capacity to move into new areas and to take advantage of suitable habitats and warming climates is completely different," says Robbin Lindsay, a research scientist at the National Microbiology Laboratory in Winnipeg. Lindsay has studied this particular tick extensively in a long career that has made him an internationally recognized expert on vector-borne illnesses. He has been bitten by hundreds of ticks, a couple of which made him hideously ill, and yet, when he speaks of *I. scapularis,* admiration suffuses his voice. "The sky seems to be the limit for them," he says. "They are taking over the reins as the number one vector of pathogens to humans. And that's only changed in the last twenty years." *I. scapularis* is "extremely catholic with its taste for blood," Lindsay says. It will feed on both migrating birds and big mammals that cover wide ranges—helping it expand its territory—and it's also delighted to encounter a human and her dog. In tick-borne disease literature, the blacklegged tick is almost universally described as "aggressive."

The knowledge that this tick is proliferating in the most densely populated area of Canada, potentially spreading not just Lyme disease but anaplasmosis and babesiosis, an infection that resembles malaria, is disturbing in ways that it feels as though we have not yet grasped. It will precipitate a significant change in how Canadians view our relationship with our environment. When I asked another tick expert, Nick Ogden, a research scientist at the National Microbiology Lab, how much he worried about ticks, he explained that, since he did much of his research in Africa, where he was thinking about puff adders, typhoid, cholera, malaria, and about a dozen other things that might kill people, ticks figured fairly low on his list.

In Canada, however, the list of ambient things we must fear is not long. Outdoors, it's grizzlies, rattlesnakes, maybe a rogue cougar if you are massively unlucky, and, of course, the cold. Otherwise, it's icy highways, drunk drivers, and unstable ladders. But we don't need to worry much about lethal things lurking in our gardens or in the dark corners of our closets. Or, rather, we didn't need to. Until now.

On a cold, grey autumn afternoon, Katie Clow takes me into the woods, an hour's drive from Guelph, to drag for ticks. She equips me with a white haz-mat suit, seals off my ankles with duct tape, and hands me a white flannel blanket taped to a metre-long stick. Then we set off into the underbrush, dragging the blanket awkwardly over brambles. We pass a few hikers, who take one look at our CSI getups and our blankets and hurry away. Clow and her team of students go dragging every year, and every year they find ticks farther north. "One year you find a couple of ticks," she says, "and the next year you're finding half a dozen ticks, and the next year you're finding ten ticks and *Borrelia*."

Where there is *Borrelia burgdorferi*, there's a risk of Lyme. The disease causes fever, fatigue, and joint aches, and it is an emerging public health problem. There were 2,025 cases reported to the Public Health Agency of Canada in 2017, the last year for which data is available, but the agency speculates that number is underreported and predicts as many as 10,000 new cases each year in the 2020s. Huge swaths of Ontario, Quebec, Manitoba, New Brunswick, and Nova Scotia are now considered Lyme risk areas. But, at the same time, we're more aware of Lyme and how to manage it: many people who spend time in areas with ticks know to do a "tick check" after being outside and know that, if you find and remove the bug within twenty-four hours of when it began to feed, you can't get the Lyme bacteria. While there is no vaccine for Lyme available, the bacteria is treatable with antibiotics. If you don't find the tick or don't get the telltale bull's-eye rash, Lyme can be harder to identify, and you can suffer symptoms for weeks or months until diagnosis. A small subset of those infected report a "chronic" infection, although most scientists reject the idea this could occur; one hypothesis is that the so-called chronic infections are actually coinfections of Lyme and another tick-borne pathogen, such as *Anaplasma,* for which doctors do not routinely test.

After about an hour in the forest with Clow, I stop for a periodic inspection of my blanket and, right near the top, heading with surprising speed for the handle (and my bare hand) I see—something? "Katie," I ask, "is this a tick?"

Clow hurries to me, leans in for a look, and lights up like Christmas morning. I have picked up an adult female black-legged tick, with a black hood on a handsome dark-red scutum. A short while later, Clow finds a tick on her own blanket and is equally pleased: you'd never guess she has encountered ten thousand ticks in her professional life. She identifies it— another *I. scapularis*—then sets it gently down on a leaf so I can have a good look. The tick immediately scooches to the end of the leaf and begins to wave its front legs back and forth.

"Ooh," Clow croons. "She's questing!"

A questing tick waits at the end of a blade of grass or leaf, with its legs outstretched, tracking the changes in heat and CO_2 that signal that something biteable is walking by, poised to jump aboard—a sort of arthropod hitchhiking. Watching

Clow watch the tick, I recognize the phenomenon that I saw in Robbin Lindsay and every other tick expert I talked to: the admiration for ticks, for their adaptability and ingenuity and complexity.

A tick can live for a few years without feeding. But, like a video game vampire, they need blood—a "blood meal," as it's known in the zoology world—to level up and move between stages of the life cycle. They start out as eggs, typically laid in the leaf litter on a forest floor. (But some, like the brown dog tick, will deposit eggs in a convenient crevice in your floor.) The eggs hatch into larvae, with just six legs, usually in late summer, although the seasonal timing varies between ticks. And thus begins the hunt for a host—a reptile, bird, amphibian, or mammal that will provide the blood that will allow them to mature. When the larvae have fed on something small, they drop back to the ground and moult, becoming a nymph. They will overwinter, burrowing under the leaf litter to keep warm. As nymphs, they develop that last set of legs, and at this stage, they can host many pathogens. When the next blood meal happens, typically off a larger creature, they are able to be infected with bacteria or viruses—and to pass them on, when they feed again, as an adult. Nymphal ticks are tiny, and thus much harder to spot and remove, so they're the ones most likely to get away with making their way inside your trousers and having a long feed. After the nymph moults again to become an adult, it quests its way onto a larger host, such as a dog or a deer or a human. Males and females meet and mate on a host before dropping off; some species lay several thousand eggs in a process that can take weeks. If a female doesn't find a host to reproduce on in the fall, she burrows back into the leaf litter and waits for spring.

It's a risky requirement, this need to feed on an exponentially larger and faster-moving host, when you're a slow-moving creature the size of a sesame seed. And it's the range of ways that ticks have found to navigate that risk that seems to make the tick people really excited. I asked Nick Ogden, a soft-spoken man from the north of England who immigrated to Quebec after studying Lyme disease at Oxford, why he chose ticks when he was starting out as a veterinary scientist—given that he had his choice of creatures great and small. He started off casually but, in seconds, had revved up into a full-throated praise song:

"They're just amazing, amazing parasites. They are immensely tenacious. You find ticks pretty much everywhere in the world, in a whole lot of different ecological niches to which they have adapted themselves. Their whole biology is fascinating, how they sense hosts around them by being able to smell the CO_2 we produce and the other kinds of pheromones that we're producing. Then there's their whole feeding thing: everyone thinks it's like mosquitoes, that they're just like a syringe, but they're fascinating! They dig a hole in us, they bury their heads in, and they feed for up to two weeks. The mouthparts of an adult female tick are about the size of a splinter. The first thing that you feel with a splinter is that it hurts. And the first thing that you feel when a mosquito bites you, either it hurts or it stings. But you don't know the tick is there!"

A tick can coat its body in its own saliva, a liquid salty enough to pull moisture from the atmosphere. That is sustenance enough to keep it going for months—or even years—while it's waiting for a meal. The saliva is produced in glands that can occupy as much as a third of the tick's body cavity, and when it is time to feed—the most dangerous time in a tick's life—this liquid is its primary defence mechanism against a host's immune system. When you stroll by and a questing tick makes the successful leap, it attaches in one of two ways: by transuding a sort of glue to keep its mouth in place, or, as with the blacklegged tick, by poking barbed mouthparts into your flesh. When a tick bites, it begins by secreting enzymes that destroy a circle of flesh and create a tiny puddle of blood, which it begins to suck up. (A tick takes in blood and sends out saliva in alternating cycles.) The tick needs to kill pain so you won't realize it's there and flick it off. And it needs to stop your body from mounting the immune response that it would otherwise send against this intruder from the moment its mouthparts pierce your skin. Among the 3,500 proteins identified in the saliva of various ticks, some stop the molecules carrying a pain signal, while others are vasodilators, to get the blood flowing, or anticoagulants, to keep it from clotting. Some proteins stop the histamine response, which would make the bite itch and clear a path for immune cells to reach the site. There are also molecules that inhibit white blood cells. And, because the tick needs to keep feeding for days—keeping your immune system fooled—it changes up the protein composition of its saliva, like a dash into a phone booth for a new disguise.

So there you are, with a tick feeding and passing pathogens into your body after having disarmed your immune system. It's the ideal situation, Ogden says, for a virus or bacterium looking to fulfill its evolutionary obligation by finding new animals to infect. "If a bug has to get from an arthropod into a host, what a wonderful gateway it is, where the tick's feeding."

Ticks like their tissue soft and thin, as Eric Stotts can tell you. Last October, Stotts went on a guys' weekend to a cabin near Port Mouton, on Nova Scotia's south shore, a couple of hours from his home, in Halifax. An affable forty-eight-year-old architect, Stotts goes with his buddies every year, and in addition to a lot of eating and drinking, they always take on a project and learn a new skill that someone in the group can teach. Last fall, it was filmmaking, and Stotts spent much of the weekend crouching and lying on the forest floor as he filmed long, still shots of the last dark-yellow leaves on the trees—aiming for what he called a "kaleidoscopic" nature effect. He thought his film turned out pretty well, and when he was back in his home office on Monday, he was feeling good about things.

Until he went to pee.

And there, on the end of his penis, was something small and black. "I kind of poked at it enough to realize, okay, it's definitely attached, it's not moving," he says. And that's when he thought, Tick. He zipped up his pants and headed to the medicine cabinet for tweezers. His wife worries about Lyme disease, so he knew the procedure: he had to make sure he got the whole tick out, including the head and mouthparts now buried in his most sensitive skin. "I had to be a little bit more aggressive than I would have hoped," he remembers. There was digging. But Stotts is the sort of fellow who likes to find a bright side, even when gouging the end of his penis with a sharp instrument. "In a strange way, I was kind of grateful that it was so obvious, you know, because, had it attached anywhere else, it could have gotten to the point where the transmission of Lyme disease could have happened," he said. "It picking the most prominent, visible spot ended up being a real advantage for me, actually."

Using Google, Stotts quickly confirmed that his new companion was *I. scapularis*. He kept the tick bits and headed to his walk-in clinic, wondering if the tick should be tested for Lyme. He was waiting in an exam room when a nurse came in to ask what ailed him. Stotts decided there was no point in trying to maintain decorum.

"I had a tick on my dick," he said.

The response was not what he expected.

"Well, that's the second one I've had this week," the nurse told him. (The other patient had actually had a tick on his scrotum, which Stotts considers far more distressing and invasive than a tick on the penis. He feels sorry for that guy.)

The doctor Stotts saw did not send the tick for testing: at this point, the protocol is to prophylactically treat anyone likely to have been exposed to Lyme disease. Stotts swallowed "horse pill" antibiotics for two weeks and sent an email to all the guys who had been with him that weekend, warning them to do a tick check.

He did not, for the record, attach a tick dick pic.

Even a decade ago, when Stotts started going on those weekends away, there were only a handful of tick populations in Nova Scotia; now, the region south of Halifax is the second-biggest source of mail-ins for Clow's pet tick study, which began last year. But the section of Canada that makes a suitable habitat for ticks—and for *I. scapularis* in particular—has expanded dramatically over the past twenty years. There is a lot of debate among scientists about why that is, but climate change figures in almost every hypothesis. Of all the environmental factors that affect the size of tick populations, temperature is the most important. Shorter, warmer winters are good for tick life cycles. It's not that they freeze in winter—they can weather the cold hunkered down in the leaf litter of wooded areas. Rather, when it's colder, a tick takes longer to quest and is slower to move through each stage of the life cycle—so a greater proportion of them die before the cycle is completed. At the same time, milder winters mean that migratory birds are nesting progressively farther north, transporting ticks with them to establish in new areas. Hardy *I. scapularis* has proven adaptable to a range of climates, from Florida to Nova Scotia.

Research conducted in the 1980s, when Lyme disease was emerging as a serious public health problem in the US, showed that most of Canada was too cold to have to worry about the blacklegged tick; Ogden found the same thing in the early 2000s. But the research reveals the speed at which the impact of a warming climate has been felt: Ogden and Lindsay contributed to a paper, published in the *Journal of Applied Ecology* in 2012, predicting that "the proportion of the human population of eastern Canada inhabiting areas with established tick populations [would increase] from 18 per cent in 2010 to over 80 per cent by 2020." And they were right, although Ogden wishes it were otherwise. "It's gone from a model-based hypothesis to a public health reality in a decade," he says. Meanwhile, the white-footed mouse, the most important reservoir for the Lyme bacterium, is also expanding its range north. It likes the short winters too, and breeds more rapidly than it used to.

And then there are other ecological factors, such as forest fragmentation: when urbanization breaks contiguous wooded areas up into patches. You might think that would reduce the amount of wildlife around and thus be bad for ticks, but by condensing the populations of some mammals (such as those mice) while evicting large predators, such as cougars and wolves, that would eat the deer that are a preferred host for adult *I. scapularis,* it creates a sort of tick food court. "We see every year this creep northward," Clow says, "where sites that didn't have ticks the year before are now positive."

On a September day in 1958, a tow-haired four-year-old named Lincoln Byers was in the barn on his family's farm, twelve kilometres west of Powassan, Ontario, when his brothers noticed his eyes were acting funny, flicking to the side, and he had a tremor in his arm. His parents took him to see the family doctor, who took one look and urged them to get him to the Hospital for Sick Children, in Toronto, a six-hour drive in those days. When they got there, Lincoln was feverish but with no obvious cause of illness. Two days later, he was fading in and out of consciousness, and monitoring of his brain suggested it was inflamed. On the fourth afternoon, he suddenly stopped breathing and was placed in an iron lung. He died two days later.

His devastated parents gave permission for an autopsy to two physicians, one of whom was Donald McLean, a virologist at the hospital who had been following the case closely.

They cultured fragments of Lincoln's brain and injected the product into mice, which developed signs of acute encephalitis. But, when the samples didn't come up positive in serology tests for any known encephalitis, McLean and his collaborators realized it was a new virus. The closest comparison they could find was a virus that, in Russia, was transmitted by ticks. So McLean hung up his lab coat, picked up a shotgun, and drove his team to Powassan. They began around the Byerses' farm and worked outward: they killed squirrels, chipmunks, rabbits, and other mammals, and harvested any ticks they found. Back in the lab, they found that some of the animals also activated the blood test they had developed for the new virus. Eventually they concluded that Lincoln, the second youngest of nine children, had likely been bitten by an infected tick while holding dead squirrels his brothers were skinning. McLean and his colleagues also tested the blood of park rangers and others who worked outdoors around Powassan, finding that several of these people carried antibodies to the virus; they expanded their investigation to the blood bank in Sudbury, where they confirmed that a percentage of the population had been exposed.

Newspapers ran alarmed stories after McLean published his research, but Lincoln's death remained a tragic exception. By 2009, fewer than fifty cases of what came to be called Powassan virus had been reported anywhere. That, Katie Clow says, makes for an interesting epidemiological mystery: the virus is clearly circulating somewhere in the wild, being passed from ticks to mammals and back again, often enough that there are these rare infections—but not a major public health threat.

The discovery of Powassan virus, a vicious form of encephalitis that can cause permanent neurological damage or death, in *I. scapularis* changes how we have to think about that risk. *I. scapularis* can pass the virus to its eggs, so its offspring do not have to progress through the life cycle and get infected to become vectors. And, while the public health response to Lyme disease is based on tick checking—because it will take the tick at least twenty-four hours to pass on the bacteria—this is not the case for Powassan. A tick needs to feed on you for only about fifteen minutes to transmit that virus, explains Nicole Nemeth, a veterinary pathologist and expert on arboviruses, including Powassan, at the University of Georgia. Lyme bacteria live in a tick's gut, and when the tick starts to feed, the bacteria begin to multiply and make their way through the gut wall and up to the salivary glands, where they are transmitted to the host. But Powassan lives and reproduces in a tick's salivary glands, so it's right there, ready to go the moment a tick bites.

Powassan virus is an arbovirus within the genus *Flavivirus,* along with the West Nile, dengue, yellow fever, and Zika viruses. While some unknown percentage of people who are infected show no symptoms at all, the virus is fatal in approximately 10 percent of diagnosed cases, and it causes permanent neurological damage in an estimated 50 percent of those who recover. In 2017, a sixty-eight-year-old retired high school teacher from Ottawa found a feeding tick on her shoulder when she was at a cottage in southern Quebec. "I'm not a hypochondriac," she says. Two of her friends had had a rough go with Lyme disease, so she took the tick to her doctor, who gave her a prophylactic antibiotic and—in a lucky twist—sent the tick off to Public Health Ontario for analysis. Reassured, the woman, who told me her story but doesn't want to be "the public face of Powassan," travelled to British Columbia on holiday.

Ten days later, in Kelowna, she developed a fever, then quickly became so ill that her partner had to drag her unresponsive body through the doors of an emergency room. Soon she was in intensive care with encephalitis and meningitis. Her children flew to her bedside because doctors warned she was unlikely to survive. Because of the known tick bite, she was treated for Lyme and tested for other tick-borne illnesses, including Powassan. But that test was negative, which isn't uncommon: the virus may not show up in blood tests for two weeks or more. The determined—and fascinated—doctor who first saw her in the ER tracked down what Robbin Lindsay, who was eventually pulled into the case, calls the "smoking tick." The specimen was rushed to the National Microbiology Laboratory, where it was identified as a partially engorged *Ixodes marxi* nymph that, when put through molecular testing, was found to contain RNA for Powassan virus.

In Kelowna, the woman, still desperately ill, looked in a mirror and saw her face, frozen and twisted like that of a stroke patient. As she was being loaded onto a medevac flight back to Ottawa, she was finally told of her diagnosis, but she was too sick to care. It was only days later that she began to process that all this had come from a tick bite. She spent two months in a rehabilitation hospital, using a wheelchair, unable to feed herself; she is back to taking long walks now but has limited use of one arm, poor balance, double vision in one eye, and experiences occasional fits of choking. "People think of Lyme and think, well, it could be treated," she says. "But I don't think that there's a big awareness of the fact there are ticks that, one bite and you could die."

The surging prevalence of Lyme disease tells us how far and how fast *I. scapularis* is moving. It will take Powassan virus with it, and other things too. "This tick is a microbial sponge," Lindsay says; it seems as though anything researchers screen it for, they find. First it was *Borrelia,* then *Anaplasma* and *Ehrlichia,* which causes fever and muscle aches. "What's so striking with this tick is that, the more types of pathogens you look for, the more you find."

Tracking the diseases is one preoccupation for Lindsay and his colleagues; they also have to be on the lookout for new ticks of concern. In August 2017, a woman in New Jersey was shearing her pet sheep when she discovered ticks. And not just a few: by the time she made it to her local public health department, she had more than a thousand ticks on her own arms and clothing. There, entomologists struggled to identify the ticks—they didn't look like anything local—and eventually Rutgers University scientists had to use DNA to establish that they were *Haemaphysalis longicornis,* the Asian long-horned tick. It is native to Japan, Korea, China, and Far Eastern Russia. In Asia, it is a source of serious illness, including a hemorrhagic fever called *Huaiyangshan banyangvirus,* which is fatal for up to 30 percent of those who catch it. *H. longicornis* was the first invasive tick species found in the United States in eighty years, and there was hope the cold winter would kill it off. But, the following spring, the CDC reported, it was found not just in the original location but in nine more states, on wildlife, on pets, in surveillance (dragging in the woods), and on two people. Clow and Lindsay say it's only a matter of time until it is found in Canada. Researchers can't tell yet whether mammals or birds in North America will be receptive reservoirs for the *Huaiyangshan banyangvirus* (it is, however, closely related to the Heartland virus, which ticks pass to reservoirs in the US) or whether the tick can transmit pathogens to humans on this continent. For now, the biggest risk is to the livestock industry. Female Asian longhorned ticks are capable of parthenogenesis: if they don't find a male to mate with, they simply reproduce alone. A single tick can quickly create infestations of thousands of ticks on sheep and cattle, and the effect can be so severe that the host dies of blood loss.

Every tick researcher I spoke with brought up the Asian longhorned: nobody likes these lurches into the entomological unknown. I asked Nicole Nemeth what keeps her up at night. "Just the ease with which these pathogens spread around the world, and we won't necessarily even know it until it's already killing either a bunch of people or a bunch of animals—that's scary, and it could happen any moment of any day," she said. "A tick on someone's body could easily then drop off and bring something crazy from the other side of the world." Crimean-Congo hemorrhagic fever, say, or Russian tick typhus.

In 2004, I was living in South Africa and travelling for work across the continent. One day I developed a terrible fever; a crusty black scab, about five centimetres in diameter, on the back of my left calf; and lymph nodes as hard as stone. A succession of doctors diagnosed me with everything from a spider bite to cutaneous anthrax to possibly leukemia before an acerbic elderly South African medic surveyed me in a hospital bed and said, "*Rickettsia africae*. Good old tick-bite fever." I soon discovered that half of the people I knew in Johannesburg had had it, usually as children. In southern Africa, the bacteria is carried by *Amblyomma hebraeum,* a prettily patterned tick that feeds primarily on cattle. It rarely passes diseases that are fatal to humans—although the fever often lasts for weeks, as mine did—but the losses to livestock are punishing in poor countries such as Eswatini, which, I eventually figured out, is where the tick got me.

I recovered from *Rickettsia africae* after forty-eight hours on antibiotics (although the lymph nodes in my leg stayed rock-hard for the next year). It remains, though, the sickest I've ever been—despite twenty-five years of reporting in countries full of all the things Nick Ogden said preoccupied him more than ticks. I never again went into long grass or paddocks in tropical countries without dousing my legs with DEET.

Yet I didn't take the same steps when I was back in Canada—not until Katie Clow took me tick dragging. She thinks about the campaigns that have, in her lifetime, persuaded people to use seat belts, quit smoking, and wear sunscreen, and she wonders how long it will take for the change to come with ticks. "My message to people is, We are in a new era where this is part of your daily public health things that you're supposed to be doing: if you go out in the woods, you should be checking yourself for ticks, you should be covering up." Tuck pants into socks, wear long sleeves, apply insect repellent, and perform a tick check—behind your knees, behind your ears, and, well, where Eric Stotts would tell you to check.

Since my day in the woods with Clow, the Canadian forest trails I have walked since I was a child feel different. In the woods these days, I get the occasional cold prickle on the back of my neck. It's not the sense that bears or wolves might be watching me. It's not the fear of getting lost in the cold. It is the knowledge that there are thousands upon thousands of tiny hunters who can sense my breath and who are waiting, poised at the end of a long blade of grass, their front legs out-stretched, for me to come close.

ALL THE KREMLIN'S MEN

On Seventy-five Years of Russian Interference

Joyce Wayne

Seventy-five years ago, three days after Japan formally surrendered, bringing the Second World War to a close, Igor Gouzenko vanished from the Soviet embassy on Charlotte Street in Ottawa's tranquil Sandy Hill neighbourhood. Over the next forty-eight hours, something of a legend was born. The details and chronology differ depending on the teller, but most agree that Gouzenko, who had been in the city since 1943, first headed to the *Ottawa Journal*. The twenty-six-year-old cipher clerk had secrets to share. But then his courage failed him and he went home.

Gouzenko, who had learned days before that he was to be shipped back to the Soviet Union, was frantic and afraid. He had stolen scores of top secret documents and worried that as soon as the embassy's military attaché, Nikolai Zabotin, discovered the missing papers, he'd be ambushed and punished.

When he arrived home, at 511 Somerset Street West, a strange-looking two-storey affair with round windows overlooking a park, Gouzenko's pregnant wife, Svetlana, urged him to try the *Journal* again. They had their safety and that of their two-year-old son, Andrei, to think about. So he returned to the paper and pleaded with the night desk to inspect his cache of documents. But the editor—perhaps uninterested, perhaps unable to understand the excited Russian before him—made one of the greatest gaffes in twentieth-century journalism and turned Gouzenko out onto the street.

On the surface of things, the Soviets and the Canadians were the best of friends. On Saint-Catherine Street in downtown Montreal, for example, Eaton's flew the hammer and sickle above its main doors, and the director John Grierson's pro-Soviet documentary *Inside Fighting Russia* had been enthusiastically screened across the country. Yet the friendship was paper-thin. Soon, the Canadian government would learn the USSR had been intent on gathering secrets from our Chalk River laboratory, a hive of scientific activity located about two hours northwest of Ottawa. As the Manhattan Project at Los Alamos, in New Mexico, moved ever closer to producing the A-bomb, the Soviets aggressively targeted associated operations here. And Gouzenko carried the proof on that sultry Wednesday night of September 5, 1945.

After his rejection at the *Journal*, Gouzenko tried the Justice Building at 294 Wellington Street. But the department was closed, and he was told to come back the next day, which he did with his family in tow. He forced his way into the inner sanctum, where he threatened to shoot himself if he wasn't allowed to speak to the justice minister, Louis St. Laurent. (For years, his pistol was enshrined in the International Spy Museum, in Washington. It was recently returned to Ottawa.) Sent away again, Gouzenko tried the RCMP's Bureau of Naturalization, where his attempts to defect were refused.

Back at his apartment—technically Russian property—he heard Colonel Zabotin's chauffeur pounding on the door. Gouzenko and Svetlana, in desperation, hid little Andrei with a neighbour, and Gouzenko jumped over a balcony to get away before Vitalii Pavlov, the embassy's *rezident,* broke into the home with a group of Zabotin's men. Only then did the police get involved. "It was like a game of cops and robbers" is how Amy Knight described the scene in *How the Cold War Began,* "with the hapless Ottawa police confronting belligerent Russians desperate to find their missing cipher clerk and his documents."

Gouzenko never did meet with St. Laurent, but he did get the attention of Norman Robertson, who contacted Mackenzie King. The undersecretary for external affairs told the prime minister that a "terrible thing" had occurred. "Robertson seemed to feel that the information might be so important both to the States ... and to Britain that it would be in their interests to seize it no matter how it was obtained," King wrote in his diary.

But the prime minister was distracted, putting the final touches on the Throne Speech and preparing to open a new session of Parliament. He was also leery of Gouzenko's intentions: "My own feeling is that the individual has incurred the displeasure of the Embassy and is really seeking to shield himself." King was a wartime supporter of cordial relations between Canada and the Soviet Union and didn't wish to rock the boat; Robertson and others, however, ultimately convinced him to send Gouzenko back to the RCMP, who then transported him to the top secret Camp X, on the shores of Lake Ontario, near Whitby. That's where Gouzenko fell into the hands of John Leopold.

Leopold was born in Bohemia in 1890 and arrived in Canada in 1912. He was five feet four and of Jewish background—two things that made it difficult for him to become a Mountie. But he spoke several languages and was virulently anti-Communist. In 1918, he managed to join the ranks. "He spent the next decade as a secret RCMP agent," Knight wrote, "posing as a house painter and working his way up the hierarchy of the radical Canadian labour movement." Just weeks after Gouzenko defected, Leopold was appointed chief of the RCMP's intelligence branch, the Special Section, where he became among the most thorough investigators of

Communist agents and sympathizers in this country—perhaps *the* most thorough.

As Gouzenko was whisked off to Camp X, King notified Harry Truman and J. Edgar Hoover, and soon afterwards the befuddled prime minister found himself on a plane to Washington. The president and the FBI director were livid. Most worrisome to them was how deeply the Soviets had infiltrated efforts to build the atomic bomb. Yet Truman, too, was hesitant to decisively expose his Soviet allies.

It wasn't until February 3, 1946, that the nationally syndicated radio columnist Drew Pearson shocked Americans by announcing that a Soviet spy had surrendered himself and confessed to a "gigantic Russian espionage network inside the United States and Canada." Pearson, a confidant of the Truman cabinet, had been leaked the information—by the president himself. What's more, according to Pearson, "the Russian agent taken by the Canadians has given the names of about 1,700 other Soviet agents operating not only in Canada, but also in the United States."

Gouzenko's treasure trove of stolen documents, some of which were released to the public only in October 2018, was the spark that many historians believe ignited the Cold War. It was irrefutable evidence that the Soviets had set up an intricate spy operation on Canadian soil—managed by the Main Intelligence Directorate, or GRU. The telegrams, letters, and handwritten notes showed that Zabotin was running the network from the Soviet embassy on Charlotte Street. What's more, they showed that an MP, Fred Rose, was operating on behalf of the Soviets from his office on Parliament Hill.

My father, Harry Vine, was born in 1904, in Nesvicz, a tiny shtetl nestled precariously on the undulating border between Russia and Poland. Like his comrade Fred Rose, he was an active member of Canada's Communist Party. Before that, in Nesvicz, he had witnessed the brutal murder of his two older brothers. When he was only seventeen, his parents sent him to Canada to cut a trail for the surviving family members, whose day-to-day existence had been inalterably transformed by the pogroms, wars, and revolutions being waged in the Pale of Settlement. My father's brother Irving and sister Fanny made perilous journeys of their own to Windsor, Ontario, where an aunt with a farm and dry goods store offered them sanctuary.

Although our family often met for Jewish holidays, weddings, and bar mitzvahs, I never heard the brothers and sisters talk about the destruction of their humble existence in Nesvicz or about the death of their older brothers. They never spoke to their children about their voyages as solitary teenagers, sailing from the port of Danzig across the Atlantic Ocean. It was not until after my father's death that I learned of the murder of the eldest brothers. My aunts and uncles happily spoke about whose kids had been accepted into medical school—never about what had ravaged the family back in Russia. Privately, my father continued to recount his adventures during the civil war that followed the revolution, and I was all ears. He seemed mesmerized by the Red Army cavalry, which stormed into Nesvicz during the post-1917 conflict. He would vividly describe a colonel who had held a pistol to his head. He ordered my father to collect the village doctor and escort him to the train station, where wounded soldiers were lying on the railway platform. Fifty years later, my father still spoke with great pride about his own bravery.

I eventually learned that two of my father's siblings had remained in what is now Belarus, while an older sister, Dvora, married a general in the Red Army and moved to Moscow, where she taught school. During Stalin's reign of terror, her husband was taken from his bed, tortured in the Lubyanka, convicted of treason during a show trial, and shot by a firing squad. The Nazis murdered the remainder of the Vine family.

Safe in Canada, my father married Rachel, from the old country. But he was restless and eager to join the growing movement of leftists during the Great Depression. He left Windsor for Montreal when his wife took ill, taking his three-year-old son, David, with him. For years, he worked as a labour organizer in the garment factories, and he was the top dog in a group of *havers*, friends who lived in cold-water flats in the Jewish ghetto in the riding of Cartier.

In 1943, two years before Gouzenko stole those documents, my father campaigned for Fred Rose, who had been born in Lublin, Poland, in 1907. While the Communist Party was technically outlawed in Canada, operating instead as the Labor-Progressive Party, Rose was a card-carrying member running against the Co-operative Commonwealth Federation's David Lewis, in a by-election in Cartier. Rose won by 30 percent (and again by 40 percent in 1945). His was a landmark victory, celebrated by Communists and sympathizers across the country. To this day, he's the only Communist to have served in the House of Commons—and the only MP convicted of violating the Official Secrets Act.

In the late 1940s, my father's life took a dark turn. His second wife, Edith Miller, died in hospital after a simple surgical procedure. She had been the head of the Young Communist League in Montreal and an ardent supporter of international Communism. When my father attempted to contact his comrades to announce her death—mostly writers and intellectuals living in the Soviet Union—he discovered many were dead or had gone missing in the gulags. Some had died before the Nazi invasion, in June 1941.

The Gouzenko revelations, along with the subsequent trials and convictions, had frightened my father as much as they disillusioned him. It was clear that Moscow had been actively undoing the Communist Party's progress in Canada. Disheartened, he returned to Windsor, where he opened a furniture store with his younger brothers.

Although my father spoke with reverence of his Montreal years, there was always an element of secrecy about why he relocated to Windsor. He hid his Yiddish and Russian books, including Isaac Babel's *Red Cavalry,* in our cold storage room—alongside hand-preserved dill pickles and sugared strawberries. Babel's short stories from the 1920s honestly portray the brutality of the Red Army and show fascinating sympathy for the Bolshevik struggle. The Soviet intelligentsia lauded him, but his days of favour with Stalin's regime were not to last. He was executed on an early January morning in 1940, just hours after a show trial that lasted a mere twenty minutes.

On those same lamplit basement shelves of ours, I discovered the fiction of Dovid Bergelson, who was also executed, on the Night of the Murdered Poets, in August 1952, during Stalin's anti-Semitic campaign against "rootless cosmopolitans." By the time I could decipher the titles on these tucked-away books, I had learned from my father that his favourite Jewish writers were all dead, murdered at the Lubyanka or in yet another fanatical purge.

What struck me as strange, even then, was my father's nostalgia for all things Russian—literature, music, dance—along with an equally powerful distaste for Canadian culture and the prime minister. This was the McCarthy era in the United States, but even here, he was endlessly fearful of speaking about his past. Once, in grade three, I stood up in class and announced that Diefenbaker was "a terrible leader." My teacher, of course, reported my outburst to my mother, Helen Marcus, my father's third wife. She detested secrecy, but my father admonished me sternly, and I was forbidden to repeat anything I heard at home.

As I grew older, my father's stories gained urgency. Around the time my aunt's husband, the Red Army general, was executed, my father had become increasingly devoted to the idea of returning to the Soviet Union. His sister Dvora was in Moscow, but the two did not communicate during the 1930s and

'40s. Mail was stopped or censored at the Russian border, and my father had no knowledge of her troubles. And then, slowly, he turned away from Communism—as did many others who discovered how Stalin had treated their friends and family back home. The dissonance between the cause he'd devoted the best years of his life to and the stark reality of Russia's anti-Semitic police state tore him apart.

In the early '30s, Stalin had promised a place for the Jews of the world—a place that might even rid Russia of centuries of virulent anti-Semitism. Birobidzhan was founded at the centre of a modern Jewish Autonomous Oblast, sitting on the Trans-Siberian Railway near the China–Russia border. But even this dream drowned in a bottomless pit of broken promises. After the war, Stalin targeted it and its Yiddish institutions that had given so many Jewish Canadians hope. (Last year, the former party supporter Sol Hermolin told me over a coffee at the Free Times Café, in Toronto's Kensington Market, that when he misbehaved as a child, his mother would threaten "to leave him behind when the family moved to Birobidzhan.")

The promise of Birobidzhan had been on the minds of many members of the Communist Party in Canada. And in 1939, only ten days after Canada declared war, they followed instructions from Moscow and publicly supported the now inconceivable Molotov–Ribbentrop Pact between the Soviet Union and Nazi Germany. The party was actively against the war effort throughout the 1940 federal campaign, even claiming that King's decision to call a wartime election was no better than Hitler's plebiscites.

Ultimately, Canada banned the Communist Party because of its anti-war position. More than a hundred prominent members, including the party's leader, Tim Buck, were interned at Camp Petawawa in Ontario or Camp Kananaskis in Alberta, or were jailed at Kingston or Hull. Gouzenko's chief interrogator, John Leopold, who'd infiltrated the party meetings in Toronto during the 1930s, testified against Buck. The crackdown had far-reaching implications. "During the Second World War," Rhonda L. Hinther wrote recently in *Civilian Internment in Canada*, "the Canadian government imprisoned, in jails and internment camps, hundreds of far-left activists." Ethnic groups were particularly vulnerable. To be a socialist from a visible, ideological, or religious minority spelled trouble.

Early in the war, Communist propaganda in Canada made a desperately precarious situation much worse for European Jews. Moscow-approved propaganda against the Allies helped perpetuate the King government's response to Jewish refugees seeking entry into the country. It must also have profoundly affected the Jewish members of the party already here. How could they tolerate and support Hitler and Stalin's non-aggression pact?

Between 1939 and 1945, Canada admitted only about 5,000 Jewish refugees. During the same period, China accepted 25,000, Britain accepted 70,000, and the United States accepted 200,000. There was a time, before the war, when Jews were barred from swimming in Lake Ontario: "No Dogs or Jews," the signage read at a Toronto beach in 1933. The same year, a riot broke out between Jews and Gentiles, at Christie Pits Park in Toronto. During a baseball game, with several thousand in attendance, twenty young people raised a large white sheet painted with a huge black swastika, and some cried, "Heil Hitler." As Cyril Levitt and William Shaffir described in their 1987 book *The Riot at Christie Pits*, "Jewish supporters rushed the flag-bearers, and pandemonium broke out. Spectators yelled 'Kill the Jews' as youths made after one another with clubs, chains, bats, and broom handles."

By the time of the riot, Torontonians were well aware of the Nazi rise to power. According to Levitt and Shaffir, newspapers "carried horrifying front-page reports of the atrocities against Jews during the first months of Hitler's rule." The *Toronto*

Daily Star "referred to the burning of books in May 1933 as a 'holocaust,' and repeated references were made in both the English and Yiddish press to the 'destruction,' 'annihilation,' and 'extermination' of the Jews in Hitler's power." Yet five years later, the *Toronto Telegram*, which opposed Jewish immigration, declared: "It cannot be denied that Jewish people as a class are not popular in Canada."

Jews weren't excluded just from swimming in Lake Ontario. After Fred Rose was charged with espionage—after he served six years in prison and was forced to return to Poland—an aura of suspicion and exclusion continued to cloak Canada's Jewish population. Julius and Ethel Rosenberg, investigated in part because of the Gouzenko Affair, were simply US *citizens* convicted of espionage. But Rose was an *elected official* who had often lunched with Norman Robertson. And many of Rose's comrades held essential jobs in government or academia. Here, through well-placed Jewish Canadians, Soviet tentacles had reached the highest levels of power.

While my father and his comrades struggled to create a socialist Canada, Gouzenko helped expose the depth of Soviet activities. Before the revelations, Colonel Nikolai Zabotin was a darling of the Ottawa diplomatic corps. He was tall, with a fine head of blond curls and a penetrating gaze. Women, especially, were mesmerized by his Red Army uniform and flawless French and English. When not trading bons mots around the capital's most fashionable dinner tables, Zabotin concentrated on Chalk River and the nuclear reactor being built on the banks of the Ottawa River. It was there that the ZEEP prototype was developed with the help of Alan Nunn May and Bruno Pontecorvo. Both physicists had joined the Communist Party in their home countries—Nunn May in Britain and Pontecorvo in Italy. And both worked under cover for the GRU, gathering classified information about Chalk River and Los Alamos. British officials had cleared both men for work at the secret atomic laboratory, likely with the assistance of the master double agents Kim Philby and Donald Maclean.

From Chalk River, Nunn May and Pontecorvo passed secrets along to Fred Rose, who kept morale high among Zabotin's ring of spies. Once, an official from the Soviet embassy even carried a minuscule chunk of plutonium to Moscow—atomic gold that Nunn May had managed to steal. Spies were also embedded in the civil service. Yet many if not most Communist Party members and wartime sympathizers were not aware of the spying activities. They were shocked by the Gouzenko revelations, even as they were considered suspects themselves. Even John Grierson, head of the National Film Board and later the Wartime Information Bureau, was questioned by the Royal Commission on Espionage, which Mackenzie King established. Careers were destroyed, lives ruined.

Twenty-three suspects were detained incommunicado at RCAF Station Rockcliffe, and ten appeared before the Royal Commission, where Gouzenko was the star witness. They were charged under the Official Secrets Act and sent to prison. Freda Linton, who once worked as a secretary to John Grierson and who was a party member close to Rose, managed to evade the RCMP by leaving the country. She was never charged, and decades later I wrote a novel about her, *Last Night of the World*.

My father once told me that party members were never sure if they'd be rounded up, interrogated, jailed. And many, like my father, continued in a perpetual state of fear long after Russian espionage ceased to be a burning issue. In my father's case, his work for the party left him clinically anxious, with bouts of severe depression, for which he was hospitalized. He sometimes recounted life on the lam, sleeping on a different sofa every night after the party was declared illegal. Until his death in 1981, he was suspicious of being detained and fearful of crossing international borders. He never failed to keep all the doors and windows locked. He feared he would be sent back to the Soviet Union, as Fred Rose had been sent back to Poland. He wouldn't be treated as a hero, he worried, but would meet the same fate as those fallen writers he so revered.

I took a year off from my undergraduate studies at Carleton University to work as an assistant to Ed Broadbent, who had won his Oshawa–Whitby riding in the 1968 general election, defeating the former Progressive Conservative cabinet minister Michael Starr by fifteen votes. Broadbent's office was on the sixth floor of Centre Block, directly under the clock tower. I luxuriated in the leather sofas and old mahogany desks and was awestruck by the parliamentary pages, who gladly brought liquor and wine to an MP's office on demand. Lunch at the parliamentary cafeteria cost a dollar.

I answered phones and wrote letters on a tomato-red IBM Selectric typewriter. My boss was a dedicated MP who tried to convince me that John Stuart Mill was more important than Karl Marx. He was a joy to work for: fair, easygoing, and somewhat indulgent of a young woman with radical ideas about politics. Once, leading up to the 1972 "corporate welfare bums" election, I accompanied Broadbent to see David Lewis, by then leader of the NDP. I'll never be sure how, but Lewis recognized me: "Are you the little guy's daughter? Are you Harry Vine's girl?" (Lewis himself was short, but my wiry father was only five foot three.) When I admitted that I was, he replied, "One iota of trouble from you and you're out. Do you understand?"

As it was, I was accustomed to keeping secrets, having been schooled by the best, and for years I made certain to never mention my encounter with him to anyone except my father. I asked why the NDP leader was so upset almost thirty years after Rose's election, and he responded by detailing how the Rose campaign was better organized than the CCF's effort.

For decades after that 1943 by-election, my father, who never was interrogated by the RCMP—or so he claimed—

argued that the information gathered by Rose's ring of spies was of no importance and certainly nothing of serious interest to the Soviets. He maintained that it was material anyone could have gleaned by reading the daily papers or reviewing Hansard. He believed the RCMP had exaggerated the case and that Fred Rose was innocent. Only shortly before his death did his views change.

Of course, it was not the case that the information collected by the Soviet spy ring was of little consequence. It was so important that Gouzenko helped trigger the Cold War and rearrange the Canadian political landscape. And it was now clear that Soviet support for Communist movements outside Russia would be sacrificed to support Stalin's government, no matter how chilling the consequences.

In 2003, the *Globe and Mail*'s Jeff Sallot interviewed Martin Rudner, then the director of Carleton University's Canadian Centre of Intelligence and Security Studies, about the Gouzenko case. "It was absolutely explosive," Rudner said, "probably the single most important event in counter-intelligence." As Sallot wrote, "Mr. Gouzenko disclosed the existence of Soviet 'sleeper networks'—spy rings consisting of secret agents recruited at early ages and kept in place for years until they attained positions from which to influence the policies of their native countries or steal important scientific, military or political secrets." And, according to documents revealed by a later defector, Gouzenko's defection "effectively paralyzed Soviet espionage efforts in Canada for 15 years."

Igor Gouzenko and Svetlana were granted Canadian citizenship and new identities after they left Camp X. Their home in Port Credit, Ontario, was under constant RCMP protection. Although Gouzenko feared that Soviet agents would assassinate him, he managed to appear on television, always wearing a bag over his head. And he kept busy writing books. His novel about Stalinist Russia, *The Fall of a Titan,* won the

1954 Governor General's Award. He died in Mississauga on June 25, 1982.

Many of the thirty-nine Canadians suspected of working for the Soviets, including the eighteen convicted under the Official Secrets Act, were Jewish, compounding the age-old trope of the Jew as traitorous troublemaker. That Jews were also responsible for the Russian Revolution became an article of faith for many. As Allan Levine put it in *Seeking the Fabled City*, "Jews were frequently portrayed in the English- and French-language press, and by politicians, church leaders, and businessmen, as dangerous Bolshevik sympathizers; urbanites, rather than farmers, who threatened the virtuous rural ideal imagined for Canada; and above all, as a 'race' that could never truly assimilate into a Christian nation."

Not long ago, I sat down with the octogenarian Solomon Blaser, to record his memories of growing up in the Toronto branch of the Communist Party. He recalled his early days at his parents' cabin at Camp Naivelt, open to Jewish members and their friends, near the Credit River outside Brampton. Paul Robeson and Pete Seeger sang for the campers, and hundreds of orators promised a better world under Communist rule. "My parents were looking for a place for their children to swim and play in the fresh air," Blaser explained. "To purchase the land for Camp Naivelt, the members asked the Ukrainian comrades to make the offer to the landowner, who never would have agreed to sell his farmland to Jews."

Levine estimates that 30 percent of Canada's Communists in the 1930s were Jewish, although other historians consider that percentage low. Regardless, the impression that they were responsible for the proliferation of Communist candidates before and during the Second World War profoundly affected Canadian immigration policy. While the US and Britain began to open their doors to Jewish refugees, Canada steadfastly adhered to its position of "none is too many" (the phrase that Irving Abella and Harold Troper used to title their land-mark 1982 book) long after the existence of the death camps became widely known in 1944.

When the detention of the Soviet spies made the headlines in February 1946, it served to entrench the wartime views of Frederick Blair, who directed immigration under Mackenzie King. Even though Blair was fully aware of the plight of refugees, he stood firm, saying no country could "open its doors wide enough to take in the hundreds of thousands of Jewish people who want to leave Europe: the line must be drawn somewhere."

As my father reached the end of his life, he expressed his disappointment with the Communist Party and the anti-Semitism it provoked. What haunted him was Stalin's doctrine of "socialism in one country," which he believed crushed movements outside Russia. During the 1930s and early 1940s, the Canadian Communist Party had played a significant role in everyday Jewish life in Montreal and Toronto, with cultural events, summer camps, rallies, and other activities. But the Jewish membership began to shrink after the war. Moscow's meddling in Canadian politics even frightened the greater, less politicized Jewish community.

At the Twentieth Party Congress, in 1956, First Secretary Nikita Khrushchev denounced Stalin and his "cult of personality." The curtain was finally pulled back on the former premier's egregious crimes. Party members could no longer hide their suspicions: the Soviet Union had been transformed into an autocratic police state. It was also a time when the Canadian parents who spoke Yiddish at home and founded Camp Naivelt increasingly encouraged their children to attend university and professional schools—while keeping their heads down. Fewer and fewer Jewish Canadians entered politics. Fewer became journalists. The trials of shtetl life and the Bolshevik-leaning poets and storytellers who narrated a rich but tragic existence were forgotten, except by those stalwart followers who tried to keep the revolution's flame burning, even after it had burned out in the Soviet Union and the Eastern bloc.

It's no exaggeration to say that keeping a low profile became *de rigueur* for the majority of educated Jewish Canadians after the war. We have not been as active in national issues and commentary as our brothers and sisters in France, the United States, or even the United Kingdom.

In 1973, when I was sharing a co-operative home with a group of young radicals on James Street, a few blocks from the Gouzenko apartment on Somerset, Phyllis Clarke came to visit. Clarke was the co-editor of *Yours in the Struggle: Reminiscences of Tim Buck,* a book she was researching at the time. She was a stern-looking redhead with tightly curled hair, and she reminded me of my father's former comrades, who would occasionally visit his furniture store, to discuss things like the 1962 Cuban Missile Crisis and the 1968 Soviet-led invasion of Czechoslovakia. Those aging comrades would speak in hushed tones of J.L. Cohen, "the people's lawyer" who defended many of the suspects rounded up by the RCMP. Clarke was Cohen's daughter, and she had devoted her life to socialism.

I stared at her, and she glared back at me. I'll never know if she recognized me, as David Lewis had back on Parliament Hill, or if she thought my New Left housemates and I were pretenders, who understood nothing about the sacrifices she and others had made in the name of the Soviet Union and international Communism.

Inspirations

Yours in the Struggle: Reminiscences of Tim Buck
Edited by Phyllis Clarke and William Beeching
NC Press, 1977

*How the Cold War Began: The Gouzenko Affair and the Hunt for
    Soviet Spies*
Amy Knight
McClelland & Stewart, 2005

Seeking the Fabled City: The Canadian Jewish Experience
Allan Levine
McClelland & Stewart, 2018

The Iron Curtain
Directed by William A. Wellman
20th Century-Fox, 1948

WRITING THE REAL

Catherine Bush

Scene 1: Several years ago I was invited by a high-end adventure travel company on an expedition to Sable Island, the thin, ecologically delicate sandbar off the coast of Nova Scotia famous for its population of wild horses and history of shipwrecks. The island had just been turned into a national park. Wondrous as its landscapes were, it was also impossible to miss the oil platforms hovering mistily at the horizon. Over an elaborate lunch in the ship's dining room, I described to my tablemates my novel-in-progress, which features an Arctic glaciologist grappling with the ecological wreckage of the world as both a climate scientist and a parent, only to be met with the defensive posture of someone with ties to the oil and gas industry: the climate may be changing, but there's no proof that humans have caused the changes.

Scene 2: A couple of years later, I found myself, one March afternoon, in a cabin on the far eastern reaches of Fogo Island, a forty-five-minute ferry ride off the coast of Newfoundland, itself an overnight ferry ride from mainland Canada. Outside, slabs of snow-covered granite, interrupted by stands of spindly and windswept tuckamore, spread to the white and ice-choked

North Atlantic. I'd skidooed in to the cabin with two brothers from the community of Tilting, and as we sat there drinking instant coffee by the heat of the wood stove in this utterly
remote place, it struck me that in my years of conversation
with people on Fogo Island about the weather, people who live
intimately connected to land and sea and air, I had yet to meet
anyone who denied the existence of human-caused climate
change. Nevertheless, many of the new houses in the village
of Tilting have been built with money made in the oil sands.

By now most if not all of us will have contended with amplified and more frequent hurricanes, weather fronts shifting
with winds so strong they topple trees, so-called hundred-
year storms and floods, droughts that keep recurring, perilous
proximity to wildfires. Likely all of you reading this accept the
science of the climate crisis: that human activity, specifically
our burning of fossil fuels and spewing of greenhouse gases
into the air, is a driver of atmospheric warming, which in the
short term amplifies weather unpredictability and in the long
term threatens ecological catastrophe, potentially bringing
about our extinction as a species.

Despite the dire warnings about the radical need to change
our behaviour, we mostly go on living in a kind of functional
denial of this climate knowledge. We fly, we drive, we cool
our overheated houses with air conditioning powered by fossil fuels, vote for political parties that support the oil and gas
industries, and console ourselves with illusions of continuity.
I'm not innocent. I fly less than many people and I obstreper-
ously ask people if they can imagine not flying at all. (I've met
one person, an environmental lawyer, who has managed this
for many years.) But I drive regularly between city and country. I navigate my own seams of contradiction, even hypocrisy.
Nevertheless, as a writer, I no longer feel capable of making art
that fails to acknowledge the climate crisis and the existential
condition in which we all live.

For six years I've been working on a novel that attempts to bring climate science and the climate crisis into a work of literary fiction alongside some of our existential habits of denial. I'm provoked by the question of what literary realism looks like at this moment, in the places I write from on this planet. How do I create a literature that feels real when so many aspects of the lives around me are premised on the most profound fictions: that we can continue to live as we do, those of us lucky enough to be able to privilege our short-term comforts and desires, indulging in the luxury of global mobility and the individual benefits of ideologies of growth and extractivism, while ignoring the profoundly destructive consequences of our behaviour, particularly for those who come after us? What does the project of literary realism, which for the last couple of centuries in the industrialized and capitalist West has largely focused on the interactions of individual human psyches within their social milieu, look like going forward? How do we represent our current reality imaginatively, and, if we're going to grapple directly with the climate crisis in a literary work, how can we do so artfully rather than swinging about with an apocalyptic sledgehammer?

I'm drawn to thinking about my own first novel, *Minus Time*, published twenty-six years ago in 1993. It's narrated by Helen Urie, a young Canadian woman struggling to come to terms with an ecologically fragile world and with an astronaut mother attempting to set a record for orbital space habitation. The novel grew out of the collision between my childhood love of the Apollo space missions and my lifelong feeling of interconnection with the rest of the living world. Even as a child, the Christian idea of human "dominion," a.k.a. our exceptionalism, made no sense to me. While her mother circles the planet, Helen's fascination with a group of animal rights activists heightens and she gets pulled into their increasingly large-scale protests as non-violent eco-warriors.

When I wrote the novel in my twenties, I saw it emphatically as a work of realism, even as my intentions were to break through the borders of a normative domestic realism that to my mind never felt real enough. Yet when I mentioned that there was an astronaut in the novel, people often asked me if I was writing science fiction, as if I'd somehow veered into the speculative even though astronauts, including female astronauts, were as real in the 1990s as they are today—one being Canadian neurologist Roberta Bondar, who flew on an American space shuttle mission in 1992. Animal rights activists and slaughterhouses were also just as real then as now, and I wanted to embed them in a work of realist literary fiction, to expand the map of the imaginary by making animal rights activists and female astronauts as real on the page as they were actually real.

A few years ago it was a commonplace to lament the dearth of writers and artists responding to the climate and biospheric crises in their work. This is changing. But the challenge of how to do so remains and, like the changes to the weather itself, only grows more amplified.

The climate crisis is both real and hyper-real, so existentially enormous it's virtually impossible to imagine. In fact, we have no idea what's coming. We have scientific probabilities as a prognosticator of looming social collapse brought on by increasing weather extremes and food and water insecurity. Yet we can only ever imagine a future based on the past, and the past becomes less a guide all the time to what lies ahead.

While the conversation about the climate crisis seems to be gaining momentum as the timeline for meaningful societal change shortens, most people still don't want to think very much about these matters because the subject is so overwhelmingly depressing. And terrifying. This makes it hard to figure out how to give climate issues an imaginative form other than as a disaster narrative that still risks being overwhelmed by the narrative arc of reality. On the one hand, nothing seems to be changing at all, so much human activity all around me continuing to ignore impacts known for decades; on the other hand, as the pace of climate disasters accelerates, the cultural conversation does seem to be shifting—witness the rise of Extinction Rebellion as a global movement and the strikes led by youth activist Greta Thunberg. How can fiction that isn't written at breakneck speed capture something of these contradictory realities too?

Here's another problem: paradoxically, the more we talk about our actual predicament, the harder it becomes to represent it imaginatively. Through repetition, the climate crisis risks becoming a cliché on the page, overburdened with overwhelming, unchanging significance—even as it simultaneously exists as an uncanny, unaddressed presence, or present absence, in many lives.

All fiction written now is climate fiction, I would argue. More usually the term refers to a genre of fiction that addresses the climate crisis directly, often within the broader genre of speculative fiction, but this compartmentalization enacts its own denials. All writers today write in relation to the climate and ecological crises, our planetary emergency, whether these things are acknowledged or not. Because this existential condition is at the core of our current reality, it infects all attempts at artistic realism. Literature is an art of navigating between presences and absences, making the usually unseen visible and reversing disappearances large and small. Yet writers also leave traces of unacknowledged absences for others to notice. Whether or not it is on the page, the climate crisis imparts meaning: its presence or absence denotes something.

In her article "Climate Change and the Struggle for Genre," which appears in a 2017 anthology, *Anthropocene Reading* (Penn State University Press), American academic Stephanie Lemenager writes: "The question of what it means to be human in this ecological moment and how to narrate the problem of 'being human' lies at the center of Anthropocene thinking." The term *Anthropocene* may be a contested one. In geological terms our impact may remain small over time spans of billions of years, but Lemenager's words can serve as a useful guide for thinking about contemporary literary realism.

William Shakespeare's play *The Tempest,* first performed in 1611, opens with a stage-racking storm. In his essay "Enter Anthropocene, 1610," American professor Steve Mentz notes that Europeans rarely encountered hurricanes before the early-modern period. Following the argument of geographers Lewis and Maslin, Mentz proposes the early seventeenth century as the beginning of this new geological epoch, one defined by a human presence powerful enough to leave a mark on the geological record, with rising global trade and colonialism as its initial drivers. Hurricanes are a New World weather phenomenon. As European navigators struggled to contend with them, Shakespeare sends one onto the stage. Audiences of the time would have seen not just a terrifying storm but something larger: unfamiliar, symbolic, epochal.

The novel I'm working on, set in an approximate now, opens with a Category Five hurricane that has churned up the east coast of North America, leaving devastation in its wake. Tugged by warming ocean water, it swerves farther north than expected, side-swiping the small island where the novel is set. Every hurricane we encounter now, in life and on the page, becomes larger than itself, literally and metaphorically, by simultaneously embodying the climatic forces that humans have unleashed, leading to new forms of chaos. In the words of American writer Roy Scranton, author of *Learning to Die in the Anthropocene* (2015), "We live in the gap between the wind and the whirlwind."

In 2006, I saw a production of *The Tempest* by the Royal Shakespeare Company, featuring Patrick Stewart of *Star Trek* fame as the magician Prospero. Deposed from his dukedom, Prospero ends up fleeing to an isolated island with his young daughter, where he seizes control of this world and all its elements. He commands the wind and waves. As the play opens, he conjures a huge storm to entrap the enemies he's lured to the island. Often Prospero is played as an aging sorcerer. By contrast, Stewart was a virile and forceful presence, hunter and autocrat, still angry as the play ends at being compelled to relinquish his power. The production was set in the bleached world of the high Arctic, which is in fact a world of islands.

Many artists, historical and contemporary, have reworked *The Tempest* to their own purposes. The play has offered strong fodder for post-colonial retellings, such as Martinique writer Aimé Césaire's 1969 play *Une Tempête,* which shifts focus to the subaltern characters, particularly Caliban, the island native enslaved by Prospero. In Julie Taymor's film version, Prospero becomes a woman, Prospera, played by Helen Mirren. The play has also been written about in eco-critical terms, which I didn't know when I began to think about Prospero, the weather changer, as a kind of proto-twenty-first-century-human, man of the Anthropocene, who, in my novel, shape-shifts into a climate scientist.

Shakespeare's Prospero, too absorbed in his books and study, is accused of witchcraft and deposed by his conniving brother. My scientist, Milan Wells, a glaciologist engaged in studying ice cores extracted from northern glaciers, is set upon by climate change deniers in a scenario that loosely follows the contours of what happened to actual scientists in 2009, in the series of events dubbed Climategate, just before the COP15 conference in Copenhagen. A server at the University of East Anglia's Climate Research Unit was hacked, and email correspondence, released by deniers, was framed in such a way as to alter sense. UEA scientists and others, including American Michael Mann, were accused of fudging data to show warming; they were guilty, deniers claimed, of perpetuating a hoax.

The events received massive mainstream press; the scientists in question, while ultimately vindicated, faced enormous short-term pressure.

My scientist, his realistic career in tatters, flees to a fictional version of Fogo Island. Here, in the North Atlantic, he discovers real subarctic flora on the island's ocean side. Every spring and summer, icebergs, pulled south from the Arctic Ocean by the Labrador current, float past: huge, sepulchral monuments to a vanishing world. While he comes seeking refuge, determined to leave the rest of the damaged world behind, he also arrives at a place where he becomes a fictional front-line witness to actual environmental disruption.

"I have done nothing but in care of thee," Prospero says passionately to his daughter Miranda. How does an Anthropocene parent, a climate scientist no less, best care for his child? His knowledge of our predicament is a burden he cannot escape. This is Milan Wells's quandary. The novel is narrated by the recipients of his troubled and sometimes troubling care: his daughter, Miranda, and the young local man, Caleb Borders, once almost a son, whom he employs. In the novel's present, both Miranda and Caleb are engaged in trying to discover what Milan Wells is up to. Is he actually monitoring the weather, as he claims, or something else? What is the nature of the mysterious field experiments that he has conducted and in which Caleb has been an unwitting assistant? Why has Milan Wells brought three younger scientists to the island, and later three more disturbing visitors: a flamboyant airline magnate, the magnate's financier brother, and an economist who doubles as a "famous" climate-change denier?

When father and daughter first arrive on Blaze Island, driving off the ferry into thick fog, Milan, intent on hiding his past as a climate scientist, elicits a promise from her: they are never to mention the word *climate* to each other or anyone else. I can't claim this as an entirely original literary gesture. In 2014,

American writer Nathaniel Rich published *Odds Against Tomorrow*, a novel in which a disaster climate modeller working for corporations confronts a New York swamped by a huge hurricane eerily similar to Hurricane Sandy, which went howling through Manhattan just as Rich was proofreading his novel. In the book Rich refuses ever to mention the words *climate change*. As he explained in a 2013 NPR interview: "I think the language around climate change is horribly bankrupt and for the most part [is full of] examples of bad writing really. Climate change as a phrase is cliché. Global warming is a cliché." I decided to create a more active void, characters who refuse to speak the words *climate change* while the weather changes around them accumulate.

When I began work on the novel, I had a conversation with the director of Cape Farewell, a cultural organization that has brought writers and artists, including Ian McEwan, author of the climate fiction novel *Solar*, on boat trips to the Arctic to confront the realities of climate change in that landscape. I told him that I intended to have my scientist contemplate climate engineering—intentional tampering with the atmosphere in order to counter anthropogenic warming. He told me I shouldn't write about climate engineering because this seductive and perhaps impossible detour from the real work of getting humans off carbon was ethically bankrupt. A dangerous fantasy. In life, I have profound moral questions about extreme forms of climate engineering. Perhaps we'll figure out ways to capture carbon. Biological carbon sinks may make sense, but injecting particles into the upper atmosphere to create a haze that reflects back solar rays in order to mitigate warming fills me with horror. Yet such plans are indeed being investigated by real scientists such as Canadian David Keith, now at Harvard. This seemed all the more reason to write about these things as a phenomenon for fictional humans to wrestle with. In fact, it felt like a necessary form of realism.

Imagine you are a climate scientist with a child; your research, gathered from Arctic ice cores, offers evidence of ongoing warming trends; you publish your data; you breach expected scientific objectivity to offer public warnings about the risks of rising CO_2 levels. When you are accused of data fraud, and abandon academia, you create a new life close to nature, teaching your child an intimate attention to the natural world and practical survival skills, which may be the best schooling you can offer her for what lies ahead. Still, atmospheric carbon levels keep going up and Arctic ice keeps melting. Can climate engineering, in such conditions of extremity, be conceptually entertained as a form of parental care by a parent determined to do everything possible to protect his child from the worst possible of futures?

Fiction doesn't need to answer this question, only pose it, and a novel poses questions by embodying them in urgently imagined bodies and consciousnesses, set in motion to confront the world through brain and gut, amid a matrix of emotion and sensation and memory. Fiction creates possible worlds and lives in their vivid particulars: this is the core of its realism. It gives body and voice to incompatible truths, to contradictions and self-contradictions. It creates experiential complexity. This is at the core of its art. Paradoxically, through little black marks on a page, fiction offers, in the words of Scottish dance artist Paul Michael Henry, "an embodied response to the situation," the situation being our predicament at this moment of ecological unravelling.

I remember being at the Climate Engineering Conference in Berlin in 2014, a conference notable for its intense interdisciplinarity, so many singular intelligences fixed on the problem of how to address rising emissions and climatic disruptions. The conference rooms were also filled with fear. One night, as we gathered in the city's Museum of Natural History surrounded by the skeletons of dinosaurs, I listened to an American diplomat who'd worked for the Clinton administration give voice to his terror. At an afternoon session, a researcher from the South Pacific grew furious at northerners for ignoring the extreme risks faced by those in the global south. Objectivity has its place, but it is only one way of knowing, one particular way of exercising brain and body in relation to the world around us. It has its own self-confirmation biases. "Science," says American ecological theorist Donna Haraway, "is a set of situated practices."

In a 2018 *New York Times Magazine* feature, French philosopher Bruno LaTour argues that the idea that we can stand back and behold nature at a distance, as something discrete from our actions, is an illusion. As he described flying over the fissured ice sheets of Baffin Island on his way to give a talk in Calgary about obsolete notions of nature, he told an audience, "My activity in this plane going to Canada was actually having an effect on the very spectacle of nature that I was seeing. In that sense, there is no outside anymore." There never has been, a knowledge that indigenous cultures in particular have sustained while Western thought insisted on human superiority and that the rest of the world was mere material for our use.

Other ways of knowing enmesh us with our own subjectivities and reveal our porousness to a world that we are never separate from. A novel is one such mode of thought, a way of querying scientific "objectivity" while inviting us into that porousness.

In choosing to narrate my novel from the perspective of two younger characters, I wanted to acknowledge the limits of my own expertise and to view climate science through the experiential lens of those who are not scientists, as most of us are not. I also wanted to embody less obvious forms of climate denial—that of a young woman strenuously protected by a knowledgeable parent, a scientist whose fears seep out no matter how he tries to hide them. How does she come to her own knowing of a changed and changing world, knowledge that she can inhabit, that is not wholly shaped by her father's terror, that offers her agency and a way to look forward? The human response to the anthropogenic climate crisis is often an intergenerational struggle, one in which, as Greta Thunberg has declared, adults often behave like children and children are compelled to hold the adults in power to account.

"Climate change, as many have observed, appears to detach atmospheric knowledge from atmospheric sensation," writes literary scholar Thomas H. Ford. "Climate is global, a statistical construction of highly abstract and mediated modes of knowledge. Whatever the weather around you at any given moment, it is never climate, let alone climate change." Yet we can and do experience change, and we experience it constantly, incrementally, disruptively, sometimes even cataclysmically. My character Miranda Wells, alert to every shift of wind direction, senses the changes that adolescence brings to her body even as she notices the new birds arriving on the island: the grosbeaks, the goldfinches, the flocks of robins. She lives through worsening storms. She encounters melting icebergs, broken off the Greenland ice sheet, whose fragments she and others gather along the shore and put in their drinks, dissolving ancient ice and air into their own bodies, as I myself have done.

We hunger for stories because by their nature they embody principles of transformation. They are temporal beings, as humans are. In a story, something changes. In older forms of poetry, a rhyme is not a word that repeats over and over but similar words that enact change even as they recall each other, scoring grooves in our memory. Confronting change in its deepest form means facing our own mortality, since for us change inevitably leads to loss and death.

But experiences of change also connect us to everything else on this planet: life forms, weather system, earth system, oceans. Even mountains weather. A novel can be a zone for activating these webs of connection, inviting us to leap not only into other humans but beyond—into caribou and hawk and lichen, into wind and cloud and ice and sea and air. To become other, become nature. A novel shifts our attention, seriously and playfully. It offers its own modes of concentration, bringing order and unpredictability together. In its very form it opens us to transformation—taking us out of a realm of endless traumatic repetition and offering up the slim, temporary, yet nevertheless real possibility of accessing other ways of being.

THE MEANING OF POOR

Frances Koziar

I used to be one of Them, and that fact will always remain with me as a brand of my privilege, like a fallen angel who can't quite hide the scars that prove they once had wings. It is a humbling truth, almost a shame, and one that my people can sense without my telling them, like songbirds that have learned too well to be wary of snakes.

People don't like to talk about money, with good reason. It's like children discussing who got more ice cream on their cone, except the differences are huge, and no parent will come along to fix them. When people do discuss money, it's usually to talk about their loans and mortgages, and how they envy the 1 percent. They rarely talk about how much they have.

I am a poor person. Someone who could, quite plausibly, spend the entirety of my life in poverty because I am too disabled to work. I am also, to defy your stereotypes, a young, excessively educated woman in my late twenties, who, apart from having a somewhat holier and less expansive wardrobe and an overdependence on my bicycle, looks indistinguishable from a middle-class person.

But saying I am poor does nothing to convey what that word means. Those who have lived on welfare or been poor for months have only glimpsed what poverty is like, comparable to taking a wrong turn into a sketchy alleyway and beelining it out of there, or having a car brush by without quite hitting you. The full transition takes a handful of years to occur, until everything you own—your coats, your glasses, your laptop—was bought in the After. Until you feel like you've been cut and pasted into the wrong scene, the wrong movie, one where everything you see is available for Them and not you.

Until you understand how little anyone cares.

But it is helpful, first, to look at what "poor" means according to the numbers, because despite some wayward opinions, struggling to afford what you want isn't the same thing as having little money.

To simplify, there are two numbers of import. The first is the lower/middle-class cut-off. Middle-class can be defined as starting at 75 percent of the median income (it can also be defined as the middle 50 or 60 percent, or 50 to 150 percent of the median income).[1] In Ontario, the median income was $35,600 in 2017[2] for an individual. Using this method, middle-class thus starts at about $26,000 per year for an individual, which is also the approximate cut-off for eligibility for social housing;[3] those with incomes below this might be said to be "lower-class." "Poor" and "low-income" also usually reference this group as well, but both of these terms are also sometimes used to designate the second group: those living in poverty.

"Poverty" is the point at which you can't afford basic necessities[4] like food, rent, and clothing. Differences in living expenses between cities or regions, the difficulty of defining "basic necessities" (including whether you're expected to rent a single room, live in a one-bedroom apartment, or have made it through the five- to ten-year wait-list for social housing), and one's assumed skill at budgeting (or lack thereof) all complicate this general and qualitative definition of the poverty line, and it is constantly being debated. In Ontario, poverty has been defined[5] as half the median income, or below $18,000 per year for an individual, though I have also seen $16,000 listed for the poverty line.

Just as it is important to know, by the numbers, when you are not actually poor or living in poverty, it is important to recognize when you are actually rich, and to consider the possibility that you might view "rich" as ordinary. If rich starts at upper-middle-class, then according to both the middle-60-percent method (using 2013 numbers[6]) and the 150-percent-of-the-median-income method (using 2017 numbers), it would start at about $55,000 per year for an individual. If that seems too low for you, then perhaps you would agree that the top 10 percent of earners at the very least should merit this label. The top 10 percent of earners make (only) $80,000 per year[7] for an individual—an income that is often considered, at least in casual conversation, as being part of the upper-middle class.

That $80,000, and $100,000, and even $150,000 a year are not considered "rich" in casual conversation, and are instead normalized with the more familiar misnomer of "upper-middle class," is a consequence of the fact that no one wants to label themselves as rich, or at least, not until they are so ridiculously rich that they can bask in it. They always want more: more security, more vacations, more classes, more space. They don't want to see that they are doing so much better than most; that they have so much that they should be giving, rather than taking even more.

"Maybe Jesus was right," I heard a multi-faith speaker say as he railed about the corruption money could cause, "when he said it would be harder for a camel to go through the head of a pin than for a rich person to get into Heaven." But he was middle-class, and speaking to a group of almost entirely middle- and upper-middle-class people as if they were all Not Rich. As if "rich" were always some phantom executive, laughing in the faces of the rest of the world.

But this silences those living in real poverty. This sidesteps classism, ableism, injustice. This pretends that middle-class is poor, and working-class is poverty.

This erases our existence.

While the numbers are a helpful starting point, living in poverty is as much an experience of discrimination as it is a number, as much a reality of being unable to afford necessities as it is the reality that no one cares.

The system itself upholds that discrimination.

Take, for instance, the social assistance and social supports hierarchy. While there are a couple of other groups of people, including those who work part-time for minimum wage, who frequent soup kitchens, the majority of us draw most or all of our income from the government, and how much we get is based on a hierarchy that reflects the degree to which we are valued or blamed for our situations.

At the top are romanticized veterans, who, at the very least, make about $19,800 per year.[8] Slightly below them—but still clearing the poverty line—are hard-working seniors, who receive about $18,300 per year[9] if they have no other income. After a substantial drop down (at these incomes, a few thousand makes light years of difference) are disabled people, who make about $14,000 per year if we can't work, because no one likes someone who can't work but at least we have a somewhat acceptable excuse. At the bottom are those who don't have a good enough excuse, and who, consequently, only get $8,800 per year[10] on welfare, an income that can make the decision between being homeless and starving a very real one. (Their kids, however, have special status because they are not to blame for the "failures" of their parents, so you'll see ads saying things like "no kid should go hungry"—with the not so subtle message that some adults should, or that it doesn't matter if they do—or "end youth homelessness.")

Students are the black sheep of this group, honorary members ascribed a title that almost never truly fits. As a general rule, students are much richer than they—or the general public—perceive them to be. Most students receive gifts from their parents, for instance—Christmas presents, birthday presents, a used laptop, a winter coat—as well as free meals when they visit or on holidays, free moving services, insurance through their parents or their school, cottage time or other free experiences; all in all, this makes most students effectively middle- or upper-lower-class rather than living in poverty, regardless of their official income. Even student loans after the fact are a sign of wealth: in Ontario, if you're living below the poverty line, you can repeatedly defer your loan payment for six months at a time without penalty, and if you live in poverty for ten years straight, the government will begin paying off[11]your student loan for you, and it'll be gone by fifteen years.

I wearily deem students, like seniors and veterans, the "rich-poors": the middle-lower class of people who fit between poverty and full-time minimum wage, who have incomes that people on welfare and disability envy.

But students and seniors are, of course, the ones who get the discounts. Their excuse for being poor is acceptable or pitiable. Their business matters.

They matter.

To some degree, these value judgments, and classism as a whole, are perpetuated in a vicious cycle: you work hard to support yourself and do fine, and yet there are others who are living in poverty; *ergo*, there must be some reason for it; *ergo*, there must be something different about them, or wrong with them.

I am reminded of a conversation I had once, when I heard a woman railing about how social assistance was a waste of taxpayer money. I asked her if she really didn't care about disabled people or seniors or veterans.

"I don't mean *them*," she had replied. "I mean everyone else: the people scamming the system because they don't want to work like the rest of us."

But I had just named the majority of the poor community: her image of poor people was like a phantom from a bedtime story, constructed from pieces of hate and fear, sewn together by ignorance.

And, without the proper communication, without the proper self-reflection and starting real conversations about how much money we all make in relation to one another, her line of thinking made sense. If we are living in poverty when so many others aren't, then there must be an explanation. We must be lazy, or stupid, or have something wrong with us. We must be different.

But the uncomfortable truth is that we're ordinary. Yes, we have more than our fair share of disabilities, abusive families, and stories of heartbreak, but we also span all ages and genders, and come from all backgrounds financially, ethnically, and educationally. Most of us look and act the same as everyone else; we just have higher levels of cynicism. We are people unremarkable enough to go unseen, and yet remarkable enough to survive: to survive the horror stories that every poor person accumulates over the years like a lacework of scars across our flesh, and the daily feeling of being unseen and unwanted that can do far more damage.

That, I think, is really what defines a "poor person"—their grit. Grit is what makes me admire the legendary few who have lived on welfare for decades, paragons for having survived both starvation and despair while the world scrapes them off their boots. "Poor person" is a brand they burn into our flesh when we are cast out to die, and it becomes part of our identity, whether hidden or flaunted like a swear word in the face of a world that has only sought to crush us, furious and proud and betrayed and hopeless all in the same breath.

But *poor*, poor is a word that is harder to define. And despite my titular pronouncement, there is no one meaning of poor. It depends on your own particular map of life, on what you value the most, and in what manner having that taken away will destroy you. That deeper meaning of poor lies in the spaces between the words, the subtle notes of feeling and injustice and identity that you can only hear after so many years of silence have passed. It lies in the ignorance of so many everyday moments, of the social exclusion that is such an ordinary part of this culture. It lies in the emotional vulnerability that can rip the tears from your eyes when you realize you can't give your kids the world, or your pets their medication. When you realize it's not only you that suffers for this injustice, but the people you love. When you look around and see that there are people just like you who benefit from the same system that cast you and yours out with little explanation, and no justice.

For those of you who have followed me here—you, the financially privileged, and you, others in poverty who just came to hear your own voice—I leave you at the mouth of this alley with a single message. Those people sitting there huddled in the shadows, wide-eyed and forgotten, weary and battered down, are you. They are you just as the trans and the black and the disabled and the abused-instead-of-parented are you. In their memories you will see your own, in their voices, the voices of us all. In their hearts, you would find someone worth loving.

Because another meaning of poor is simply Other. The outcasts. Those who must be different, because aren't we all? Those whom we have all contributed to casting out of a system that has never been fair.

Some have been lost to hate and bitterness, but that too is justified, understandable: to be held with compassion given the hell they have been forced to live. Others are reaching out their hands, callused and bony, for yours. Hope that someday the world will change is the tiny fire on the grimy stones beside them, those wavering flames that have been their only warmth through the long dark of the years.

I cannot speak for them, but I am one of them.

FRANCES KOZIAR

Notes

1 https://bc.ctvnews.ca/how-do-we-define-the-canadian-middle-class-ubc-prof-weighs-in-1.2215851

2 https://www.statcan.gc.ca/tables-tableaux/sum-som/l01/cst01/famil105a-eng.htm

3 E.g. https://www.cityofkingston.ca/residents/community-services/housing/social/rgi-eligibility

4 https://lop.parl.ca/content/lop/ResearchPublications/prb0865-e.htm

5 https://www.thestar.com/news/gta/2016/05/09/ontarios-poverty-gap-soars-as-welfare-rates-stagnate.html

6 https://www.macleans.ca/economy/money-economy/are-you-in-the-middle-class/

7 http://www.cbc.ca/news/canada/who-are-canada-s-top-1-1.1703321

8 http://www.veterans.gc.ca/eng/services/rates

9 https://www.canada.ca/en/services/benefits/publicpensions/cpp/old-age-security/payments/tab1-1.html

10 https://www.toronto.ca/community-people/employment-social-support/employment-support/employment-seekers-in-financial-need/ontario-works-rates/

WONDER WOMEN

The Fight for Female Superheroes in Hollywood

Soraya Roberts

On a good day, to someone like me, superheroes are a juvenile distraction, like deep throating a box of Nerds when you're old enough to know better. On a bad day, they are a capitalist virus, multiplying across the culture and eclipsing everything in their path. Maybe it's conceivable for one good guy to destroy one bad guy, but how does one person—even one person with all that power—fix a world whose enemy is itself?

The day I spoke to Supergirl, May 30, a global pandemic had pushed the American death toll past 100,000, protests had broken out across the country over the killing of yet another Black man, George Floyd, and the US president had tweeted, "when the looting starts, the shooting starts." It sounds like the ideal setting for a superhero to suddenly materialize and clean house, but that's not how it works. One bad apple is not responsible for this dystopia, this is a corruption embedded in our soil.

So maybe it was the world that was cloudy and not the Zoom call that was blurry when I spoke to Helen Slater. Either way, she looked mortal in a way I didn't remember her in 1984, when she starred in the first-ever female-led superhero movie. Instead, I remember her in *Supergirl* as white-blond, bowl-eyed, diaphanous, the kind of soaring Aryan beauty that can only be created in captivity, or at least with a lot of bleach and blusher ("I'm Jewish," Slater says). More than thirty years later—me 40 and not 4, her 56 and not 19—Slater's hair is still long and light, but it isn't white. She wears heavy-framed glasses that she keeps punching up her nose. She says her daughter is teaching her about fourth wave feminism and that she is studying mythology. Slater is grounded in California, but she might as well live right next door. Because at this moment she is as impotent as the rest of us.

White supremacy, patriarchy, transphobia, every other phobia—the roots of inequality have so invaded the core of society that the very notion of a single solution, let alone a superhero to provide it, is not just a fantasy, it's an affront to reality. And yet we are overrun by superheroes. They are predominantly white men, though some superheroes of colour have recently emerged; more persistently celebrated, however, seem to be the women, most of them white, as though female-led superhero films are the last bastion of feminism. And with the December release of *Wonder Woman 1984,* it's impossible for me not to think of *Supergirl,* which was released in 1984, two stories with identical time periods made thirty years apart. It's impossible not to think about how much has changed and how much hasn't. Women still don't own superheroes, of course, but are superheroes even worthy of them?

You would think that the decision to make the first female-led superhero movie would be a monumental one. You would think that, but only if you thought that way. The kind of people who think that way aren't usually the kind of people who make those kinds of decisions. Businessmen make those kinds of decisions. And, sure, some businessmen are culturally inclined, some can think abstractly. But a lot of them don't. A lot of them think in money and that's it. In Hollywood, those kinds of businessmen (and they are usually men) care about movies insofar as movies mean box office. A good movie makes good money, a bad movie doesn't. Those are the kinds of men who made *Supergirl.* "For us, as producers," Ilya Salkind told *Film Comment* in 1983, "the point of making a film is that movie-goers looking through the newspaper pages in any big city will want to see ... one film!"

The Salkinds were a kind of producing family dynasty. Grandfather Mikhail worked with his son, Alexander, the money guy, and his grandson, Ilya, the creative one, on *The Three Musketeers* and *The Four Musketeers.* It was on that set that Alexander, whom Ilya described to me as "crafty" with money, became infamous for being the first producer to shoot two films at once (the Salkind Clause was subsequently cre-ated by the Screen Actors Guild to keep one contract from being stretched across two projects). In 1974, Alexander and son were looking for a new project when, out of the blue dur-ing dinner one night, Ilya said: "Why don't we do Superman? He's got power, he flies, he's unbelievable!" To do that, the Salkinds had to get the rights from DC Comics. Ilya called the process a "pain in the ass" involving months of negotia-tion and even a draft of the script. In the end, though, they secured the rights to Superman for twenty-five years. And not just Superman.

Supergirl isn't as old as Superman. Kara Zor-El first appeared in Action Comics in 1959, two decades after her cousin, as a kind of secret sidekick with similar powers—superhuman strength, speed, flight. While she was created by men, she did enter an industry already occupied by Won-der Woman. And if Superman is the Übermensch, Wonder Woman is the Überfrau. She is the female superhero with which all other female superheroes are compared. It's common knowledge now that psychologist William Moulton Marston created Diana Prince (who was drawn by suffrage cartoonist Harry G. Peter) in 1941 as a kind of catch-all antidote to com-ics' toxic masculinity. She appealed to lefties because she was an immigrant from an all-female island encouraging women to use their powers to act in solidarity for peace. She appealed to righties because she was a conventionally attractive white cisgender heterosexual who uses violence to get her way. "She combines multiple ideologies in one body so anyone can see in her what they want to see, and that's, I think, what makes her so popular," explains Professor Carolyn Cocca, author of *Superwomen: Gender, Power, and Representation,* whose latest book, *Wonder Woman and Captain Marvel: Militarism and Feminism in Comics and Film,* was released in August.

Supergirl had to wait until the late sixties to become the lead, by which point feminism was in its second wave. This culminated in Gloria Steinem throwing Wonder Woman on the cover of *Ms.* magazine in 1972. Four years later, the most accessible female superhero in the world would get three seasons of her own television show, with a couple of caveats. As producer Douglas S. Cramer put it, "She should be built like a javelin-thrower but with the sweet face of a Mary Tyler Moore."

That would be Lynda Carter. In her starry trunks and scarlet bustier, both of which got skimpier as the seasons progressed, her Wonder Woman became the iconic female superhero. Despite the character's activist origins, however, ABC didn't take her particularly seriously. *Wonder Woman* was clearly satirical. It had a super-cheesy theme song—"In your satin tights,/fighting for your rights"—used comic book–style speech bubbles, and its pièce de résistance was a ridiculous transformation involving a slow-mo beep-laden twirl. "Please, whatever you do, don't ask me what I think of women's lib," Carter told *Orange Coast Magazine* two years in. "I've heard that question so many times I could scream." It was a good way to avoid explaining why the first time we see Diana, she is running through a jungle in a gauzy pastel teddy and big hair like she's in *Valley of the Dolls.* "There's a reason it's called jiggle TV," says Cocca. "There's a lot more running than you need to see." Which is not to say *Wonder Woman* did not touch on feminism—it couldn't really avoid it. "Any civilization that does not recognize the female is doomed to destruction," Diana says in the pilot. "Women are the wave of the future and sisterhood is stronger than anything." It's just that she says it while torturing the woman beside her.

Superman III was "a disaster." Ilya tells me this no fewer than three times, with the same flattened *gravitas* each time. It was bad enough that the Salkinds chose to start a Supergirl franchise instead of continuing with Superman—it seemed to be less about wanting to make *Supergirl* than about not wanting to make another *Superman*. Everything about the way *Supergirl* was made signalled her second-class status. While the budget for *Superman* was $55 million, the budget for *Supergirl* was $35 million. While the director of *The Omen* made *Superman*, the director of *Jaws II* made *Supergirl*. While Christopher Reeve was paid $250,000 for *Superman* and *Superman II* (amounting to $125,000 each), the actress hired to play Supergirl was paid only $75,000. When I brought up the comparatively low fee to Ilya, he remained unfazed: "I mean, she was totally unknown."

That part is true. Helen Slater had just graduated from a performing arts high school when one of her agents put her forward for Supergirl's best friend while the other suggested her for Supergirl. "I don't want to go up for the friend, I want to go up for the lead part," Slater remembers thinking. So, her mom sewed her a costume, including a cape. "I remember feeling very self-conscious that I had maybe gone too far," she says. But she had brought a copy of *Moby-Dick* to the audition because she was supposed to be reading it during her scene and she remembers casting director Lynn Stalmaster commenting on that. It was one of the "little signposts" that told her she was doing well, despite the nerves. To get an idea of what all this looked like, you can find images online from Slater's 1982 screen test. Despite the big hair, the cheesy red headband, and the bib-like cape, she looked as earnest as she would onscreen.

The moment Slater was cast as Supergirl was actually caught on film because a documentary was being shot around the production. "I probably cried, right?" she says. No, she didn't. She appears surprisingly poised, in fact. The footage shows Slater being called into an office, ostensibly as a farewell, when the news is sprung on her. "It seems you have the part," she is told. "Really?" she says. "Oh my gosh. Oh my God. Alright." Slater explains that she came from a school that considered theatre the be-all, not television or film. She didn't think she was the best actress, nor did she think this was the best part. But she knew it was big. "The feeling was just so much excitement that I might be able to make a living at this," she says. In press from the time she looks perpetually awestruck. In behind-the-scenes footage, she is wide-eyed. Slater was so wide-eyed, in fact, that she didn't question the quality of the script ("You feel you've been chosen for something," she explains, describing her younger self as "compliant"). Nor did she question Faye Dunaway being given first billing. Presumably Dunaway was also paid a lot more, though Slater doesn't begrudge her own low salary: "For me, that was more money than I could ever imagine."

Though Slater grew up in a "broth" of strong women—an activist mom, an academic stepmom—she was only nineteen when she was cast as Supergirl. And this was the Reagan era, the era of the conservative backlash to second-wave feminism. As Slater put it, "I still felt so much of my identity and what mattered was how men viewed me." To get an idea of how they viewed her, consider *People* magazine's December 1984 issue. In an article titled "My Dinner with Supergirl," Scot Haller writes about Slater's chest growing through workouts and inquires whether she thinks Supergirl has sex. "What a strange question," the actress replied at the time. When I bring up the interaction during our interview, Slater doesn't remember it.

What she does remember is making the film itself. "It had a male director, it had a male writer, it was male producers," she says. "It was very female diminished in a lot of ways." Set footage bears this out, showing a good number of the male crew on set (including director Jeannot Swarcz) shirtless in jean shorts. In the middle of them all, Slater is in head-to-toe Supergirl regalia diligently performing her duties.

"Helen's beautiful, but not threatening to other women," Ilya said on the *Supergirl* press tour in 1984. It was another way of stating the persistent unofficial rule in Hollywood that all female protagonists must abide by: be relatable. It was actually less about Slater being non-threatening to women, more about her being non-threatening to men—where Superman was strength and power, Supergirl was elegance and style. Whatever feminist gains Wonder Woman, and protagonists like Princess Leia and Ripley, had made, the eighties' conservative retaliation against progressive movements as a whole helped ensure that female superheroes didn't get too fierce. This backlash, the plummeting newsstand sales of comics, the rise in specialty shops to fill the void, and a loosened comics code all converged to create an exclusionary fan base that, according to Cocca, was "older and more male and more white." This demographic increasingly preferred hypermasculine male superheroes and hypersexualized female superheroes—basically everything they couldn't have. Moving into the nineties, comics got even more hostile for women, the art more pornographic, the stories more violent. An *Archie* reader forever, I remember visiting Toronto's Silver Snail comic shop when I was a teenager in the nineties. I always felt out of place. And I never went in alone.

There was a twenty-year gap between the first major female-led superhero film and the second. In the intervening years, the circumstances hadn't much changed. In 2004, *Catwoman* was as much of an afterthought as *Supergirl* had been in 1984.

It was also a spinoff, this time from *Batman,* and, after a decade in development hell, it was rushed into production when another Batman movie—*Batman vs. Superman*—was dropped. The Batman series had reintroduced nineties audiences to Catwoman, but director Tim Burton's retelling was still very much within the realm of comic books' fantasy world. It was Marvel, first with *X-Men* in 2000, then with *Spider-Man* two years later, that relocated superheroes to modern-day reality. *X-Men* may have had three male stars, but it also had four significant female superheroes, most notably Halle Berry as Storm. A year later she would become the first (and only, so far) Black woman to win an Oscar for Best Actress (for *Monster's Ball*). Three years after that she would lead her own superhero movie and be the first Black woman to do so. Unfortunately, the movie was even worse than *Superman III.*

Catwoman shouldn't be as bad as it is. The budget was a healthy $100 million. A couple of women were behind the scenes this time—Denise Di Novi was one of two co-producers, and one out of its six writing credits was playwright Theresa Rebeck—and the star had just won the most prestigious acting award in Hollywood. Yet somehow all of this still coalesced into a third-rate music video. French director Pitof (yes, he goes by one name) never once lets us forget he is an effects guy, zooming and panning across every scene to the point of regurgitation. The flimsy plot has Sharon Stone fully camped out as a beauty brand ambassador shilling cream that turns your face to rock. Berry, meanwhile, seems to have aimlessly wandered off the Dolby Theatre's red carpet into the role of a meek "ugly" graphic designer whose ethereal beauty fails to be constrained by a few errant strands of hair and some baggy tunics. Her self-actualization requires being thrown off a viaduct and swarmed by an army of cats, which turns her into a half-naked, wall-climbing femme fatale.

Catwoman paws at feminism—"Catwomen are not contained by the rules of society," Berry's character says—but this soft-core fantasy is still bound by the limits of the male imagination. The film is very much an expression of a popular brand of feminism from the early oughts, just as *Elektra* would be a year later (another spinoff afterthought rush job, this time from Marvel's *Daredevil,* with Jennifer Garner playing a bustier-clad assassin). While real activism could be found that year in Washington's birth control march and in personal blogs by a diverse array of young women, popular culture preferred a more photogenic brand of lipstick feminism. Practitioners performed their sexuality as a means of subverting male strictures on women's bodies, except that their behaviour happened to play into the very male gaze it claimed to be challenging. As Ariel Levy writes in *Female Chauvinist Pigs: Women and the Rise of Raunch Culture:* "Proving that you are hot, worthy of lust, and—necessarily—that you seek to provoke lust is still exclusively women's work." Has a male superhero ever been asked, like Elektra, if he has time to get laid? Female superheroes may be immortal, but the Gods remain men.

The failures of *Catwoman* and of *Elektra* became a self-fulfilling prophecy—the work that featured women was not as good, which, as Marvel's CEO later made explicit, proved that work that featured women was not as good. In the meantime, Christopher Nolan changed the superhero genre for good in 2005 with *Batman Begins,* followed three years later by *The Dark Knight,* which gave superheroes real *gravitas,* which made them worthy of cinema. That same year, 2008, with the brighter, wittier *Iron Man,* Jon Favreau made certain there would be no turning back. Because of them, Marvel and DC and everyone else was suddenly all about the IP. If you have the good fortune of not knowing what that stands for, it's intellectual property, which is to say, any idea or character or story that already exists, that has in some sense been tested already (see Batman, see Iron Man, see any other comic book character in existence). And as you run your way down the IP, from the most popular superhero to the least, from Marvel to DC to everyone else, you are working predominantly with male characters because those are the ones that were originally pushed.

Well, DC had Wonder Woman. She had done well on television. In 1976. But a movie? There was no successful precedent for a female-led superhero movie. And Hollywood needed one. Hollywood is one of the most precedential industries around. Even if that precedent is often misguided. "Conventional wisdom is so easily proven false, it's really a conventional fear," explains Cocca. "It's based on how we devalue women so we assume men don't want to watch women, but we value men, so we assume women will watch men." Hollywood is risk-averse, it needs certainty, at least a little bit, and there was nothing that suggested a woman-fronted superhero movie could be successful. *Alien?* No, that was a sci-fi movie. *Terminator,* too. *Xena? Buffy? Alias?* TV, TV, TV. But female-led superhero movies? They all bombed.

"Where are all the female superheroes to save the world?" Hannah Gill asked in the *Scotland Herald* in 2004. Three years later, *Mother Jones* reported on "the new wave of feminist fangirls" who had their own websites and "hate nothing more than when real-life problems like the glass ceiling intrude on their escapist fantasies." As the oughts chugged along, this generation of feminists brought a backlash to the backlash, signalling that progressive movements were back on track. Online growth meant comics were accessible outside exclusionary zones, and with the boom in superhero movies and series, the audience broadened, conventions became more inclusive, and that more diverse fan base became vocal on social media. "When you put all those different kinds of pushes together, you do start to have the hiring of more diverse people behind the scenes," Cocca says.

That's where Melissa Rosenberg comes in. In 2010, her gritty series based on the Marvel comic *Alias* was supposed to appear on network television (a less risky proposition than film). Superhero Jessica Jones had a dead family and functional alcoholism and a knack for investigating. She was also goth hot and super strong and could jump really high. ABC passed in the end, but after Disney ransacked its IP to make a bunch of shows leading up to its miniseries *The Defenders,* Rosenberg was recalled. Her updated pilot, which has more than a passing resemblance to the hard-boiled teen cop show *Veronica Mars* (precedent!), hit Netflix in late 2015. *Jessica Jones* starred Kristen Ritter in a hoodie and combat boots and was praised for its handle on trauma.

If *Jessica Jones* owed *The Dark Knight,* the new *Supergirl* TV series owed *Iron Man.* Set to premiere the same month as *Jessica Jones,* CBS moved its launch a month earlier. Once again, the show was somewhat reactive, with co-creator Greg Berlanti basing his version of Kara on Ginger Rogers, who "had to do everything Fred Astaire did but backward and in heels." Like *Iron Man, Supergirl* is high on gloss and high on quips, though Supergirl herself has the same doofiness Superman did way back in 1978. She also preserves the dregs of male fantasy. Star Melissa Benoist expressed discomfort with her character's signature micro mini, while Supergirl has often been accused of pandering to feminists. (A little less sophisticated than *Jessica Jones,* this series includes lines like, "Supergirl? We can't name her that! Shouldn't she be called Superwoman?") But while *Jessica Jones* was cancelled last year, *Supergirl* remains afloat (its sixth season, airing next year, will be its last, but a new spinoff, *Superman & Lois,* replaces it). Television executives seem to prefer their female superheroes in line with their predecessors. That Helen Slater appears in the *Supergirl* series as Benoist's foster mom only underscores the proximity of the past.

While *Superman* took place in a big city and a bustling newsroom, 1984's *Supergirl* was restricted to a small town and a smaller school. Even its sexism was banal: the heroine narrowly avoids a sexual assault pretty much the second she arrives on earth, her school friend cautions her not to show off her smarts, she is saved multiple times by a himbo, and in the final standoff, the worst insult Supergirl can conjure up for Selena, the woman trying to kill her, is that the older woman has no friends.

Though planes were flown over Cannes to announce *Supergirl* just as they had announced *Superman,* the latter made five times its budget at the box office, while the former made less than half its own. Film critic Roger Ebert seemed genuinely disappointed by Supergirl's mishandling. "There's a place, I think, for a female superhero," he wrote. But it wasn't 1984. Slater thinks one of the reasons the film didn't fly was the gendered expectations around the genre: "It was really coming up under the veil of the Superman movies and male superheroes." And while she would have loved for it to have been a success (and, presumably, to have made the two sequels she was contracted for), she wasn't too broken up about it all. "I remember the feeling being that I'm not going to get stuck the way Chris got stuck," she says, referring to *Superman* star Christopher Reeve. "I felt genuinely that I got away with the best possible scenario. The movie didn't do so great, but I still got in the door enough that I could keep working."

No wonder 2017's *Wonder Woman* took forever to get here. In 2007, a Joss Whedon feature based on the character was reportedly cancelled and, in 2011, a David E. Kelley pilot was too. In 2013, DC Entertainment president Diane Nelson said that Wonder Woman was a priority but "we have to get her right, we have to." While the cancellation of *Batman vs. Superman* cursed us with *Catwoman, Batman v Superman* made *Wonder Woman* possible. Released in 2016, *Batman v Superman: Dawn of Justice* was the first time Wonder Woman appeared in a live action film. She took the form of Gal Gadot, who, like Lynda Carter, was a statuesque former model. As an Israeli expat, Gadot (who had also appeared in four *Fast and the Furious*es) had served time in the army, a detail both Hollywood and the press couldn't seem to get enough of. She was a dream come true for the superhero genre: a kick-ass supermodel. And though she appeared onscreen for less than five minutes and only had a handful of lines of dialogue (her grunts take up more screen time), she left a lasting impression.

"I think she deserves grand cinema," director Patty Jenkins says on the *Wonder Woman* Blu-Ray. Jenkins had in fact pitched a *Wonder Woman* movie in 2010, a story that centred around Steve Trevor, the pilot who crashes near Diana's island, but DC passed. Instead they went with an origin story conceived by *Batman v Superman*'s director (Zach Snyder), one in which Steve acts more as Diana's chaperone to 1918-era Europe. DC initially hired Michelle McLaren to direct, but "creative differences" sent them back to Jenkins. She pitched Wonder Woman as the ideal universal woman, not unlike Superman for men. She wanted to make something that hearkened back to the first modern superhero film, Richard Donner's *Superman,* the implication being that this would be the long-awaited first modern female-led superhero film. And it lived up to the burden. *Wonder Woman* is exponentially better than any of the female superhero movies that preceded it. It has a better script, better direction, better effects, better acting. It is grandiose, transcending the pages from which it was born, just like *Batman Begins,* just like *Iron Man*. But as Wonder Woman's mother tells her, "Be careful in the world of men, Diana, they do not deserve you."

There appeared to be a concerted effort not to make *Wonder Woman* about politics, which is to say not to make it about feminism. That makes sense if you want to appease fan boys, but it makes less sense when you realize fan boys appear to consider any progressive change political. Discrimination is also political. And fourth wave feminism is here whether Hollywood likes it or not. So, when Jenkins says of Wonder Woman, "the idea of sexism is completely absurd to her," the same cannot be said of *Wonder Woman*. None of the choices made in the film have been made in a post-sexist world. It says something that the most powerful women on Diana's island are white and that Diana was not conceived by her mother out of clay (as she was in the comics) but by a man and a woman. It says something that the friends Diana fights alongside are not women (as in the comics) but men, and that the enemy she fights is a man, not a woman (as in the comics). Diana in the film is also quicker to violence—Jenkins has said the most important scene for her was the war scene—than she ever was on the page. In Cocca's words, "They tried to centre this female character, but they got nervous about it."

Captain Marvel was designed to be Marvel's "big feminist movie," star Brie Larson told *Entertainment Tonight* two years ago. The film's release on International Women's Day in 2019 was in line with this plan. That this release date was the culmination of various scheduling conflicts with male-led superhero films gets closer to the truth. As opposed as its approach to politics was from *Wonder Woman* and as tonally different as they were, *Captain Marvel* wasn't so dissimilar. The heroine here also wore red and blue and gold and was also a soldier and also had a boyfriend in the military. "Both of them are created to be feminist, but both of them are also created to be militarist," says Cocca. Captain Marvel and Wonder Woman are alike for a reason. It's hard enough, beyond their superpowers, to distinguish male superheroes' individual personalities onscreen, but it's even worse with the women, who always seem to be a generic mix of vulnerability and strength. But either you're an individual or you're an everywoman, and an everywoman has a better chance of representing the underrepresented.

Two months before *Wonder Woman* premiered, Anna Boden and Ryan Fleck—the duo behind the indie films *Half Nelson* and *Sugar*—were announced as the co-directors of *Captain Marvel*. Boden, the first woman to helm a Marvel Cinematic Universe film, tells me they were fans of the 2013 independent film *Short Term 12,* in which Larson played a supervisor at a group home, and always wanted to work with her. "It's her humanity, you know, and how in touch she is with her emotional world," Boden explains, "and that in combination with a super-powerful hero got us really excited to tell a story about somebody who maybe was trying to push that part of themselves down." At the same time, they didn't want their movie to be too serious. I asked Boden if that Marvel CEO email from 2014—the one in which Ike Perlmutter cited *Supergirl*, *Catwoman*, and *Elektra* as reasons not to make more "female movies"—was added pressure for them, but she said no. "We felt pressure to make something good," Boden said. "I think that all Marvel directors feel a lot of pressure to make a movie that is successful because all their movies are successful and you don't want to be the one that just like completely fails."

Captain Marvel is good enough. It takes a character that was introduced in 1968 as a love interest and turns her into a fully formed heroine whose pugnacious alien side is at odds with her tender human side. Larson is funny and charming in a way that reminded me of Chris Pratt in *Guardians of the Galaxy*. The musical cues were similarly jukebox, if a little more glaring—playing No Doubt's "I'm Just a Girl" during the huge fight scene was a little on the nose—and it does hammer on a lot more than it needs to about Carol Danvers's mortal sensitivity. *Captain Marvel* doesn't announce itself in quite the way *Wonder Woman* did, but it ultimately passed the billion-dollar mark, even if it didn't make a huge impact beyond that. Still, it's hard to gauge exactly why Boden and Fleck are not involved in the sequel; Boden seemed to be weighing her words very carefully when I asked about that. "I can't say exactly, it's just that we're"—long pause—"moving on to doing other stuff." And then the publicist abruptly ended the conversation.

This is supposed to be the year of the female superhero, and maybe so, but what does changing the gender of a well-established genre really mean? From Supergirl to Jessica Jones to Captain Marvel to Wonder Woman, the players may have changed, but the game remains the same: the men made the rules, now the women are just operating within them. Is it even that many women, anyway? While fan outrage makes it seem as though superheroines are taking over, per Cocca, "it's a really really small change, you know, numerically." Film, television, comics, each of these media only has women starring in under 20 percent of its titles. That may be a 300 percent growth from a decade ago, but that doesn't mean the representation is fair, it just means it's slightly less unfair than it was. Hollywood may want to diversify its audience, but not at the expense of the old one. That means you start with white women, maybe some men of colour, but women of colour? They may make up the majority of earth, but they make up the minority in superhero movies.

The only way to keep female characters from being burdened, from being basic, is to have more of them. That way each one doesn't shoulder all the pressure of representing an entire gender. But to have more of them, there has to be more diversity behind the scenes, so that homogenized groups of executives at profit-oriented companies are not making all the same decisions. "While there are a number of popular, strong, complex female superheroes," Cocca writes in *Superwomen*, "in general what we see is underrepresentation, domestication, sexualization, and heteronormativity." But I don't want to sound too pessimistic. It is something to go from 19-year-old Helen Slater being given one shot at Supergirl by a man to 34-year-old Gal Gadot co-producing and starring in a four-film Wonder Woman franchise directed by a woman. And despite the pandemic, a number of female-led superhero movies are still set to go in the next few months besides *Wonder Woman 1984*. Cathy Yan's recently released Margot Robbie vehicle *Birds of Prey* was followed in August by *The New Mutants,* an X-Men spinoff starring Maisie Williams, while Cate Shortland's *Black Widow* starring Scarlett Johansson is still on Marvel's slate. Not to mention Chloe Zhao's *Eternals,* which will be fronted by Angelina Jolie and Gemma Chang in 2021, and talk around the role of the *Black Panther* potentially being taken over by Letitia Wright following Chadwick Boseman's sudden passing. Female superheroes are so in vogue right now it's virtually impossible to keep on top of which ones are coming when and how and with whom in charge.

But in case you're getting too excited, as one of those barely considered last questions I sometimes absently put to sources, I fully expected Cocca to laugh off my pessimism when I asked what there was to say there wouldn't be, at some point in the future, another backlash. "Nothing," she responded flatly. "Certain people have to prove themselves over and over." Oh.

Supergirl may be one of the weakest superhero movies around, but it still has one of my favourite scenes of any superhero movie ever. It's a moment around fifteen minutes in that was absent from the release I saw as a kid. In it, Supergirl has just landed on earth. After zapping open a daisy with her eyes (just go with it), she discovers that smelling that same flower sends her floating above the ground. Delighted, she wiggles her red-bootied feet and squeals as she stretches her arms wide and her chest out and floats from rock to rock, before gliding for a long spell through the trees. Slater was on wires to shoot this scene, which only really allowed her to move her arms, but several months of practice results in an entrancing "flying ballet" that has her gently swooping upside down and around, her primary colours popping against the comparatively drab landscape and seventies music. As opposed to contemporary superhero films where everything is amped to the extreme, Supergirl's juxtaposition against this prosaic backdrop makes her movements, her figure all the more magical.

It's unfortunate that when TriStar pushed to make *Supergirl* shorter, according to Ilya, this is what was cut. It's unfortunate that what remains is Supergirl predominantly using her powers in the context of conflict, rather than in stolen moments of peaceful solitude like this. Because at a certain point you have to question the very idea of the superhero at all. The idea of the exceptional individual, whose superiority manifests in their power to combat and to destroy. Even Supergirl herself finds it unfortunate. "It would be great for me, selfishly," Slater says, "if we saw more, in the spirit of feminism—true feminism—just a wider range of women carrying the mantle that are not necessarily vaulted or held up for their ability to conquer."

She'll have to look beyond *Wonder Woman 1984*. The sequel to *Wonder Woman* is about the greed that led us to where we are today, sure, but it is also made within an industry that is itself a symptom of that greed. Diana returns in Reagan times to face a Trump type (Pedro Pascal) against a backdrop that is now a trope of retro pop culture: the eighties mall. The film's release was originally pushed to October 2 in the midst of the pandemic, which you could argue is because it looks better on the big screen. But, again, it's really about the numbers. It's more lucrative to have a theatrical release than a direct VOD release, as together they allow a costly film like *Wonder Woman 1984* (budget: $175 million) to profit. Which may be why, pushed again to December 25, in a climate that is seeing very few people in theatres, the film will still premiere simultaneously onscreen and streaming on HBO Max (a move which was reportedly made to bolster the fledgling service, though international markets without HBO are restricted to a theatrical release only, from December 16 on). Regardless, with the industry's ironclad hold on superhero product, I haven't been able to see the film. Even *Vogue,* which featured Gadot on its May cover, was only shown half an hour at the Warner Bros. lot (for all of that, *Vogue*'s verdict—"it is an all-encompassing and visually stunning (and quite loud) experience"—tells us nothing).

In an interview with *Collider* in December, Jenkins took pity on her public and revealed that the Orwellian date of the title doesn't just serve as a setting for *Wonder Woman 1984* but as a metaphor for today, in which our excesses have virtually sunk us. "I was like, What does Wonder Woman—if Wonder Woman is half God and is wise and kind and loving and generous in this way—what would she say about our world right now? How would she encounter that?" From what I can tell, she encounters it much as she has encountered everything else, with a lot of kicking, lassoing, yelling, and bullet dodging, leaving plenty of destruction in her wake. But perhaps that's the big joke. That the tagline, "a new era of wonder," for a film set in the past, in the end reminds us that we are doomed to repeat ourselves.

THE FINCA

Eva-Lynn Jagoe

The first notes of Federico Fellini's *Amarcord* soundtrack emanate from the hi-fi. My uncle plays it loud, when the heat has diminished and a cool breeze sweeps through the house, carrying with it the salt of the Mediterranean and the pine of the mountains. The sound echoes in the cavernous high ceilings, spreading out through the arched windows and into the garden, where my mother is deadheading geraniums, inhaling the pungent scent of the broken stalks. As soon as we hear the music, my cousins and I leap into motion. I grab little Alicia, who giggles with giddiness as we glide across the tiled floors, other kids jumping and skipping and shimmying past us. Uncle Tony grabs Leonora by the waist and spins her around as she bats at him with a dishtowel. My grandmother, who will be dead in two years, sits in her armchair, Mickey, the fat dachshund, farting at her feet, which tap slightly under her long blue gown. Pepi and Joaquín come to the doorway and laugh, which makes me theatrically dip Alicia backwards and give her a swooping Rodolfo Valentino kiss.

Years later, I watch Fellini's film, and see the images that danced through the minds of my family members as we children danced to the music that summer of 1979. Set in a village that could be the one near our finca property, *Amarcord* affectionately portrays its inhabitants through the seasonal variations of a year in the 1930s, mixing fascist realities with adolescent daydreams, sexual initiations with death and departure. Remembering my teenaged brother's overt fascination with his godmother's cleavage, Leonora and Tony's screaming fights when they both got drunk and threw plates at each other, and the sickening smell of incense mixed with cologne and body odour that permeated our local church as the priest droned his litany in Catalan, I now understand why my mother would say, "Our lives are like something out of a Fellini movie."

We are not, however, a family in a Fellini film. We never have been. We only lived the fantasy version of it through Tony's curation of us. He, a British art dealer who moved to the Costa Brava in the 1960s, saw us through his expat eyes, fetishizing the grand old mansion, the passionate anger, the simmering discontent, as components of a Spanish life that he wanted to live. So he made us paella and invited bohemian artists and scattered large stone and iron sculptures on the grounds of the estate. We liked this version of ourselves: a charming, degenerate bourgeois family who summers in the decaying splendour of a villa decorated with taxidermied animals, larger-than-life oil studies of flamenco dancers, dark carved furniture, and Andalusian coloured tiles. Merchant Ivory meets Salvador Dalí, with Nino Rota music animating it all.

Take away the framing device, however, and we turn out to be a lot less flamboyant than we seemed that afternoon. Housewives scrutinizing Princess Stephanie of Monaco in *¡Hola!* magazine, men reading the right-wing newspaper, kids watching too much badly dubbed *Little House on the Prairie*—much of the time spent in that house did not live up to its grandeur. See the chubby girl, her rainbow-striped jeans and her uneven pigtails, arguing with bratty Marcos about whose turn it is on the bike? That's me. I'm doing a pretty good job of cussing in Spanish.

But really, I am just the American kid who lived her entire suburban fall, winter, and spring longing for the light and colour and beauty of another finca summer. Fluent in Spanish, I am not from a Spanish-speaking country. My mother tongue is very directly learned from my mother, who has not lived in Spain since 1956. I grew up immersed in a language that was private and intimate, that was connected to my mother's birthplace through the only location I knew: that mansion outside Barcelona.

My Spanish is not only geographically unrooted, it is also temporally anachronistic. Since it came from a woman who was not living her language in the present, it is marked by the lingo of another era. The turns of phrase that I learned at home in Maryland were hilarious to my Spanish cousins, who said I sounded like someone out of a Franco-era radio novel. I spent my summers trying to take on intonations and slang that were more current. The most shameful thing to me was to be American, known for being loud-mouthed, badly dressed, and uncouth tourists abroad. The second most shameful was to be old-fashioned, to say the equivalent, in Spanish, of "gee whiz" when all the cool kids were saying "gnarly." I never fully managed to pass. In Madrid, people thought I was from Barcelona, but in Barcelona, people could never quite place me. My inability to speak Catalan, which was so politically urgent in the post-Franco years, marked me as an outsider, or, worse, as a Spanish nationalist.

One night, in my thirties, in Argentina, giddy on wine after having spent an evening gossiping with my friend Daniela, I took a taxi home and I finally managed to do it, I passed as a *porteña* as I talked to the driver. I felt like I was channelling the Argentine accent, the almost Italian lilt, the *vos* form of address. For that finite time of the cab ride, I played my role to perfection. In Spain, however, my long intimacy and history with my family make it so I can't just perform a part. I want to speak like they do so that my roots will be as deep as theirs in the soil of the arid mountains that surround the finca, so that I belong to a place that, to this day, fills my dreams with its graceful arches, with its cool marble staircase. Dreams which, I've been told by roommates and lovers who hear me talk in my sleep, are always in Spanish.

With the COVID-19 crisis, my family in Spain and I are in touch daily. Much of the WhatsApp chats are taken up with memes and jokes. But the other day, there was a video that my cousin sent of my aunt Chichi. I visited her last year in the Canary Islands, where she now lives in an advanced state of dementia, and she was only able to say a word or two, seemingly incapable of verbal interaction. In this video, however, Chichi chatters as she sips her tea. I watch it over and over, mesmerized by the language. The way that she punctuates her short bursts with a brusque *sí, sí* makes me think of the staccato diction of wartime news announcers. Chichi speaks the Spanish now that I spoke as a child, full of dated mannerisms and sayings.

In the eight-minute video, she answers questions posed to her by a neighbour, whose thick Canary Island accent contrasts with Chichi's crisp Continental tones. When asked if she wants to go visit the finca (a cruelly ironic question, since our family is embroiled in a lawsuit over the property and none of us will ever see it again), Chichi says dismissively, "*Sí, sí,* we can go," but she's not interested in planning for the future. What she wants is to dwell in the past, the deep past of her own childhood, in which she and my mother would play hopscotch in the garden. In her mind, the *masover*'s daughters, crowded into the sixteenth-century farmhouse, are waiting for the little señoritas who come every weekend to fill the big house with house guests and lapdogs and maids in uniforms. The *masover* and his family have not lived there since he was imprisoned by Franco's troops, but in her mind there is no interruption of the civil war. The finca waits, unchanging, for her weekend visit.

Chichi's nostalgia is uncanny to me, because it so closely resembles my own. Until I listened to her reminisce, I had not known how much the finca pulled at us all, the heavy house a repository of history and memory into which we poured our different fantasies and yearnings. I had thought it was just me, on the other side of the Atlantic, who missed it, who had what we now call FOMO (fear of missing out). When I arrived in the summers, it felt like everyone else had always already been there, living their exotic Latin lives and speaking their ever-evolving and shifting language. In reality, they had just gotten there a little before me, enough to take the white sheets off the furniture, and inspect the damage to the electrical wires made by the wintering mice. Enough to make the finca feel time-lessly present, which is how we all liked it best.

It is, of course, not timeless, but very rooted in a geopolit-ical context of resource extraction and stark social inequality that spans the centuries of its existence. Even in the brief moment of the Second Republic, when it seemed that another political order was possible, the finca still imposed hierarchies. According to my mother, the only reason the finca was passed over in the anarchist attacks that swept the area after the civil war erupted was that people in the village respected my British grandfather. She says that, after they went into exile, her uncle arranged for a "Communist top official" to live in the finca, knowing that this would protect it from "vandals and wartime thieves." The life of leisure that we all got to live every summer was predicated on a class privilege that was brutally asserted throughout Franco's forty-year dictatorial regime.

Listening to Chichi makes me, in the grey Toronto spring of isolation, rewatch *Amarcord*. Her anachronistic language returns me to Fellini's cinematic language of nostalgia. What strikes me the most this time around is that in the year *Amar-cord* depicts, some things change, but many don't. No one gets visibly wiser, or grows up into adulthood. There is no one central character. Instead, a full cast of characters animates the setting, a village which is, in its nostalgic evocation, the main attraction.

For years, I saw myself as the main character in a drama of seasonal exile. That is how we tell ourselves stories—we place ourselves in the centre and look for the narrative arc. Fellini, at the height of his directorial prowess, knew how to narrate a story that didn't need to focus on one person, a story that could be a depiction—loving, critical, realist, tinged with nostalgia—of *a place* and those who inhabit it.

Watching the characters congregate in the central plaza of *Amarcord*'s village, I see that I was just one member of the cast called family, all of us yearning to be back on the set again so that we could, for the brief months of the summer, be larger than life. That set, with its dusty pink stucco and the cool shade of the linden tree, shaped each one of us, from my long-gone grandmother to my ninety-five-year-old aunt to my own sons, who only got to go there once, but who still talk about it. We all dream of the finca, and of who we got to imagine ourselves to be within its gated walls.

THE MEDIUM
OF THE ARCHIVE

Elizabeth Dauphinee

I.

At the Cenotaph, an old man with a thin wisp of a voice clutches his cap against the wind and looks around at the small collection of people who still think about the war. His words are completely drowned out by the ear-splitting chop of a passing motorcycle. I look beyond him and down the hill. Behind the sharp whip of the wind, the lake is a warm autumn sapphire. I step closer to the small staging area at the foot of the Cenotaph where the other old men in military uniforms stand as close to attention as their sagging bodies will allow, waiting their turn to summon their ghosts.

I hear fragments now.
"…heroes"
"…sacrifice"

The poetry of Czesław Miłosz skitters across my mind—

We, saved by our own cunning and knowledge
By sending others to the more exposed positions

Urging them loudly to fight on
Ourselves withdrawing in certainty of the cause lost ...

Blessed are those that survive.
That is the first anti-beatitude.

Walking up the uneven brick path to my crumbling house, I feel its embrace. When it comes into full view, my heart leaps as it has only ever done for people—for my sons, for example, or their father. I love the watery stain of its porch lights, the warm glow of its lead glass, the carpet of sugar maple leaves littering its crooked fall garden.

When I saw it for the first time, I thought it too big and dark—a bulky brick Victorian with a closed layout that didn't let enough light into its honey-toned rooms. But even the realtor marvelled at the stained glass transoms over the bedroom doors—each one a pair of fleurs-de-lys in lead-lined fields of pale pink, violet, and cerulean. It was hard to admit to myself that the reason I wanted the house was its stained glass transoms, so I seized on the idea that its walking-distance proximity to the planned Allandale Waterfront commuter station was the reason I should buy it. It would be an investment. And, I could take the train to the university where I work. But it was the transoms that lured my attention away from all the problems with the house that were plainly apparent—like the fact that it had broken windows, a cracked concrete porch, and a woefully outdated electrical panel. Those things should have brought me to my senses. But, instead, I lay awake at night listening to the sharp sounds of midtown Toronto, and the expansive house an hour's drive north would creep into my thoughts. I couldn't shake my feeling of desire.

Considering all the things that were obviously in need of repair and having no idea how much any of it would cost, I offered forty thousand dollars less than the asking price and the house was mine. It didn't take long to regret it. Slowly but surely, the deep damage of time and neglect began to reveal itself. It was worse than I had imagined. None of the outlets were grounded; the windows—even the ones that weren't broken—were drafty in winter; the eavestroughs were failing; the subfloor in the downstairs bathroom smelled of mould; the waste stack was cast iron; the sewer was clay; the waterline servicing the house from the street was galvanized steel. When I took down the haphazard panels of drywall in the basement, I saw that the block foundation was crumbly on the south-facing side, where the water sits and freezes and expands.

I can never pay for all these things, so I manage the catastrophes one at a time, and the balance on my line of credit ticks up another two thousand dollars, or another three. I service the debt, and so grow accustomed to living in this precariousness. It is tempting to think about selling it. After the Allandale station is built and the commuter trains are running, I start to get fliers in the mailbox from developers and brokerages.

We buy houses!

I can call this number. They'll pay me cash. But every time I contemplate it, I look at the stained glass transoms, and I withdraw to hope for another year without a disaster. Sometimes I keep these fliers for a while—like parachute cords—but I always throw them away. I line the modest parlour with books on war and ethics. I light the wood stove and I think about the long history of shelter this house has provided for its generations of people. I grew up in a house older than this one. In the attic, along the oak beam that ran the length of the roof peak, people had carved their initials.

You will outlive me, say these engravings to the house.

At night, I stare into the glow of the firebox and I feel the temporariness of it—the fragility of my life's configuration—health, hot water, economic and political security, juridical peace.

The house offers up its first artifact in July, right after I move in. The toilet leaks in the tiny bathroom under the stairs and destroys the subfloor. The water also wicks up the hundred-year-old plaster, and the walls have to be torn out. In the quiet heat of the early afternoon, while cracking out chalky chunks of horsehair-reinforced plaster, I find, stuffed in an electrical box wedged inside a hole in the lath, a half sheet of folded yellow newspaper. The corner is torn and the date is missing, but I know it's from 1945 because the photograph is iconic—The Big Three: Churchill, Roosevelt, Stalin—plus Molotov, at Yalta. I smooth it out on the floor with my plaster-dusted hands. It has the smell of the university's library, the smell of disintegrating paper and thirst.

Left to right at Yalta farewell dinner are Secretary of State Stettinius, Stalin, Roosevelt, Churchill, Molotov.

The Yalta Conference—Birth of the Veto—Plan for Division of Germany

Triumph and Tragedy

I consider these global architects. They look smug. Remorseless. There is no trace of the sixty million dead that made their world possible.

The projector reel that begins to roll in my mind is the only medium of the war's archive for me. My access to it is limited to this. Piles of skeleton-bodies, the forest of dead at Katyń, the siege of Stalingrad, gas chambers, ovens, the barracks at Auschwitz and Dachau, the firebombing of Dresden and Tokyo. Our perverse inheritance, rippling out into oblivion as it is absorbed and diffused by generations concerned with newer crimes. I think of the fragment of the Gospel of

John that sits on display in a climate-controlled chamber at the University of Manchester. It is the earliest known piece of that Gospel—the evenly spaced, wide Greek letters set out on a scrap of tea-coloured papyrus just large enough to offer this:

And Pilate said to them, "Take him yourselves, and judge him by your own law."

I used to visit that tiny Greek fragment when I was a lecturer there at the Centre for International Politics. It sits inside its airless chamber, an emissary from another world. I don't know how to think about what that fragment offers us—a splintered admonition? a blueprint for a way of life? an instrument of war? I know that history is not linear, but I don't know how to think about it in a different way. I teach these things to students without understanding them myself. My mind folds up like a paper accordion trying to think about it.

I frame the fragment of the Gospel of Yalta and prop it up on the narrow table in the front hall.

The rhythm of academic life rises and falls in semesters: fall and winter; fall and winter; fall and winter, punctured by the occasional summer course or sabbatical. From the peaks and troughs of this life, I research and teach and try to write for my field's professional journals and presses.

In summer, I wake in the morning to water the lace-cap hydrangeas that I keep wishing I hadn't planted. I planted them because they remind me of my mother, but they're not native here, and they struggle in winter. I wanted them to remind me of the things she loved—the nodding towers of huge-headed blue hydrangeas on the oceanfront in our small town where we used to hold hands and walk at night—the smell of the salt on the east wind. Sometimes I get homesick for her, and sometimes this affects my judgment. So, I keep watering them with my critical eye, wishing they were blue instead of pink and hoping in a funny way that they'll just die so I can move on.

I'm standing among these hydrangeas when the guy from the city's Heritage Committee appears from around the corner. He stops to say that he's walking around the neighbourhood, encouraging people to put their homes on the municipal heritage registry. "The first block of homes near the new station has already been bought up by a developer," he says. "They're going to be tearing them down to build condos and commercial space," he says. It is part of what the city Planning Department calls the "intensification of the Essa Road corridor."

Our red-brick century homes fan out in blast-radius fashion from the old Canadian National station lands where Allandale Waterfront stands today—the station that justified the purchase of the house as an investment rather than a moment of madness. The station itself is meticulously reconstructed to its original appearance, an imposing building with long, lead-lined windows and an Austrian-looking watchtower that makes me think of concentration camps.

The huddle of smaller homes of the yardmen, firemen, and conductors gives way, up the hill and past the churches, to a second line of bigger brick vernacular Victorians and Gothic revivals, the homes of locomotive engineers and supervisors. Their class divide—evident in their size and ornamentation—notwithstanding, the mortar lines on the brickwork bear the imprint of the same pointer's tool.

"Put your house on the heritage registry," he says. "Protect it. It means any developer you sell it to has to wait sixty days instead of thirty to demolish it."

I want to laugh.

"I'll look into it," I promise. But I didn't think I would.

As he leaves, he turns and says, "Did you know there was a pilot that lived in your house?"

On teaching days, I slip out the front door and walk the short distance to the train. The new station glows radiant against the bay in the rising sun. Southward towards Toronto, the forests on the Metrolinx line are stained November ochre. The sun rises in spectacular shades of pink and purple, dappled with streaks of glowing silver clouds. Fallow fields are being levelled for housing developments. From the train window, in the ruins of a clear-cut forest, I see a turtle picking its way across the destruction. Month after month, through the window of the train, I watch the landscape change. I watch fields and forests being cleared and foundations being poured. A little while later, I see the matchstick pressed-wood frames, the Tyvek insulation wrap flapping in the wind. I watch the traffic congestion and the commuter platforms grow and swell. The two tall apartment towers in the distance in Vaughan become three, and then five. I start to look more closely at the houses along the line that look like mine, red-brick turn-of-the-century Victorians standing like orphans amid huge industrial zones full of derelict vending machines, dumpsters, and shipping containers. The house I love best stands like a sentinel between two container yards at Highway 7, its tight lawn and neatly stacked firewood like a rebuke from a stubborn past.

The idea of the pilot keeps returning to me. After a while, I go to the place where academics go when they're bothered by ghosts, the archive. I find his father first, John Randolph Patton, and the house, in the municipal tax records of February 1909. I find his obituary. Born in Fergus, Ontario, in 1872, John had loved gardening and poetry and his wide circle of friends. The archivist locates a photograph of him with the Brotherhood of Locomotive Engineers at the Allandale train yards in 1919, the year that Canadian National took over the prosperous line. John stands third from the left in the back row. He retired in 1937, the year that some say was the last chance to avoid the war in Europe, without ever having had an accident on the job. I extrapolate from this that he was a meticulous person. But maybe he was just lucky. I frame the photo of the Brotherhood standing together in front of the old Allandale station and I put it with the Gospel of Yalta.

What is at stake in how we tell a story? Everything.
Everything is at stake.

Archives lead to more archives when the generations being
logged are the sons of Empire. So, of course, I find the pilot—
Jack Patton: J-15106—in the digitized archives of the Royal
Canadian Air Force and, later, in the UK National Archives.
At the recruitment intake in Toronto, in August 1940, he was
described as a "good, sincere type. Average pilot material." In
November, the remark: "Tries hard, no outstanding strengths
or weaknesses." At Uplands, in Ottawa, a glimpse of his embodiment in the notation: "This airman's height as indicated in
medical reports will not permit him to be gunner or observer.
If he does not make grade as pilot—will have to remuster to
ground duty."

rks 500.   Marks Obtained 420.... Percentage 84...... Passed or Failed......P......

Position in Class..31.........   No. in Pilot's Class......65....................

Good sincere type.   Average pilot material.

Second Recommendation: This airman's height as indicated in
medical reports will not permit him to be gunner or observer.
If he does not make grade as pilot -- will have to remuster to
ground duty.

rds Cffice

When he volunteered himself to the RCAF in 1940, he was
a grocer's clerk on Essa Road, the same road at the centre of
the city's intensification project. Every day, from our house,
he would have walked to that job. Every day, from our porch,
he would have looked down the street towards the CN yards
where his father had spent his career, first as a fireman and
then as an engineer. There's no point in speculating about
why he volunteered to fly fighter planes. Maybe that was its
own explanation: flying fighter planes. The archive offers up
an aerial photograph of a crowd at the Cenotaph in 1939.
A bi-wing WWI plane is parked there. I will learn only later

that the RCAF sold itself to worried parents as a much safer service option than infantry. But it turned out that the average life expectancy for a fighter pilot was thirty days, the same measure of time the developer has to wait before tearing down that pilot's home.

I call my insurance provider to ask about putting Patton's house on the municipal heritage registry. They respond that our relationship will be severed. They don't offer a "heritage product." I argue for a few fruitless moments and then give up. So, I apply to put it on the "non-designated" list, which does not provide the extra thirty days' protection from the developer. Thirty days is semantics, anyway. I go to the Heritage Committee meeting with a PowerPoint presentation—photos of the baseboards, the rosette window, the old-growth pine pocket doors, and, of course, the transoms.

My application is approved, and the city dispatches a photographer from *Barrie Today* to take a picture of the house. When he comes to the door with his big camera, I start telling him about the pilot. He stays to write a story on the house.

The story is broadcast, and it seems the house uses it to begin gathering its things back to itself. It's like something has broken down between our worlds, like a crack in a pane of frosted glass. Things come rushing in, beginning over the course of a three-day rainstorm.

I open the door to a woman standing on the porch, the rain teeming down off the balcony behind her. She looks nervous.

"I saw your story," she says. "I lived here. I lived in this house."

She peers beyond my shoulder into the house and then looks back at me. She seems like she is not sure why she has come.

"Would you like to come in?"

She seems anxious, but she agrees. We move slowly through the rooms, and I fill the nervous silence with talking, about the little flooded bathroom under the stairs, the wood stove, the drafty windows. We walk up the creaky stairwell to the landing on the second floor and she lingers there for a moment, looking at the balcony door. Suddenly, she turns to me.

"Do you find the house to be haunted?"

My heart pops up in my chest. "What do you mean?"

"Up here. On the landing. I had a daybed. Whenever I would sleep out here, I would sort of see her, or feel her. A woman . . ." She trails off, shaking her head. "That's why I left. My daughters couldn't stand it."

She doesn't stay long, but she leaves that behind.

The very next day, an artifact arrives. It comes wrapped in newspaper in the arms of a man who says he is the grandson of Jack Patton's cousin Dorothy. Her younger sister, Kae, had—like Jack—been born in 1916. I will see a grainy snapshot of Jack and Kae together on a beach in North Bay cottage country only later, their arms slung around each other's shoulders at the water's edge.

Now, on the threshold of Patton House, Kae's grandnephew stands holding an official framed RCAF portrait of the twenty-four-year-old Jack. His silk wings are affixed to his lapel, his cap peak pitched at a formal angle that makes a pale-haired child look more like a man.

"My mother read your story," he said. "She thought you might want this. It's been in her basement for seventy years."

He reaches into a cloth bag and pulls out a folded newspaper. It is the same ancient colour as the Gospels of Yalta and John.

Looking at these artifacts, I wonder about how the edges of time must come up against themselves, and about how they must sometimes fold over, creating creases that were not there before, thresholds that allow connections to be made between otherwise incongruous times and spaces. I start to dream that I am living in such a crease, and that the house is a boundary between these edges of time. But I cannot see across it. I can't see that other world.

I think the Pattons must be on their side of the crease, reaching for us, too, and that this might be what the woman who said the house was haunted had heard.

I hang the portrait of Jack with the Gospel of Yalta and the photograph of the Loyal Brotherhood of Locomotive Engineers. Looking at the photographs together, I start to think about the role of the house, of the position it holds in space and time, it is here and now, but also somehow not; it is also somehow with another time, with other people; it is *otherwise* across dimensions. I start to think of the house as an archive.

"Someone brought these while you were away!"

The girl next door who feeds my cats when I'm away comes flying across the front gardens clutching a stuffed manila package to her chest.

"They came from British Columbia!" she says breathlessly as she speeds up the cedar steps. She stops short and offers me the package solemnly, with both hands. "British Columbia," she repeats.

I don't know anyone in British Columbia. I went there once, when my grandmother died. She died unexpectedly, on her way to the opera. By the time I arrived, she was curled up like a tiny, desiccated mummy in a hospital bed.

I reach out and take the envelope. "I don't know anyone in British Columbia . . ." I murmur. But she is already gone, whirled on her feet and down the steps and back across the garden.

Inside the manila envelope is a portrait of Jack more informal than the one his cousin had brought.

And there is a smaller portrait, a family portrait, the first photo I ever see of his mother, Jessie, and sister, Mary. Jack is in his mother's arms, an infant in a white lace gown. Maybe it's his baptism photo. Despite the formality of the portrait, Jessie looks to me like she wants to smile. John stands beside them with Jack's five-year-old sister, Mary, on his other side. She wears a gold bracelet on her wrist and a chain with a locket

around her neck; signs of working-class wealth—like the stained glass in the transoms and over the picture window.

The third photo is a portrait of the house itself with what looks like a wedding party on the porch. It is undated, but the gardens at the base of the porch look like new plantings, suggesting it is from around the time the house was built, maybe even its very first summer, in 1908, which was also the summer that John and Jessie married at the Burton Avenue United Church.

I frame these things. The hallway fills with the portraits and artifacts of a family that is not mine.

In the amber light of the hanging lantern, I stand and stare at them, straining to find them in my own inheritance, in the peace that I only know how to teach as an absence of war, in the children I am raising towards an equivalent destruction, in the edgelessness of the grief that underpins the post-Yalta world. We set people in the firmament as examples of something else. We reduce them to the instruments of freedom and necessity. We repeat their crimes and the crimes committed against them, unaware of the simulation. The Yaltas do not end. And the ritual resurrection of the dead that takes place at the Cenotaph stitches them all into the service of war's necessity.

Just before Remembrance Day the following year, the guy from the Heritage Committee stops to ask if I can share the RCAF portrait with the city so that they can place it, along with the portraits of dozens of other people who didn't come home, on a banner on the lakeshore. He will become an adornment on a windswept corner, an ornament of the state.

But he is not merely these things. His mother makes that clear as she holds him in her arms with her quiet, content smile. He is not a hero or a sacrifice.

He is her afterlife, extinguished.

I try to imagine how it could have been worth it for her.

II.

My father named one of his horses Biggin Hill, after their RAF station." The wing commander's daughter serves tea from a china pot in her living room in Waterloo. I have driven across the Creemore highlands to see her. She has seen the photographer's article in *Barrie Today,* and she writes to say she has a silk handkerchief and a locket that Jack sent to Mary for Christmas in 1940. "With Love & Best Wishes."

He was still in Canada then, at the Elementary Flying Training School #13 in St. Eugene, Quebec. She lets me photograph the locket and the velvet box with his handwriting inside. She lets me touch his silk RCAF wings.

She shows me a portrait of her father. I recognize him from the squadron photos, from before he was its commander, and

I can see him in the features of her own elegant face. She shows me a photograph: men running across a snow-dusted field, their breath coming in fine clouds.

"This moment," she says, "is an exclamation point in what is otherwise an orthography of waiting. It is punctured by reading. Playing chess. Writing letters. Getting drunk. My father never talked about the war," she says. "But he screamed at night in his sleep."

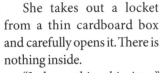

She takes out a locket from a thin cardboard box and carefully opens it. There is nothing inside.

"Jack sent this to his sister," she says. "And she didn't ever put a photo of him in it. Why?"

It's a helpless question. But there is something about the image, a pink Spitfire that seems to be plummeting into the sea, that makes me wonder whether the locket might have taken on an unbearable quality for her after his death.

In a certain way, memory is erased when stories are told. How can the wobbly fragments of broken memory, how can disconnected artifacts and grainy photos, compete with the seduction of a plot-driven narrative? And that war story, told often enough, becomes cliché. In a war with sixty million dead, cliché is maybe all that is possible. But here, in the pilot's house, through the medium of its archive, I can hear other things, the flow of rain from the roof, the creak of the floorboards, the quiet of the house without him. At the bottom of the stairs is a massive oak finial crowning the top of the ornate post. The wood has the silken sheen of a hundred years' worth of passing hands rounding the corner, Jack's hands and Mary's, Jessie's and John's.

I rearrange the photographs. I strain myself towards them. I feel the fullness of their lives, their desire to be something more than what I am able to say of them.

On Remembrance Day, the city sets Jack Patton's portrait on a nine-metre banner near the foot of the lakeshore in old Allandale. When I see him for the first time, the wind is whipping up a stinging rain and I feel a shrinking in my heart. It bothers me that he's out there in the cold like that, people driving past, not knowing who he is. I don't want him to be an example of his fate, but I also don't know how to make the long filaments of his silence mean something more.

How does the past live in us, even without our knowing it? This thing the old men at the Cenotaph call a sacrifice, what is it, really? They gave up more than just their lives. They think that sacrifice lies in the past, and that we should remember it so that their deaths will have been justified. As Empire builders know well, the martyr's death is a powerful weapon. But that loss goes on and on, made partly in the silence of the generations that will never be born; generations that will never exist. We have never seen them, even though they live with us. They are our ghosts.

In my file folders and drawers, and hanging on the walls of Patton House, are only snippets of paper, photos, and annals that resist anything but the most fragmented of interpretations: "severely reprimanded" at RAF Peterhead in October 1941 for "using a service vehicle without permission."

A letter to his parents, dated April 1, 1942, is addressed to our house on William Street. Part of it was published in the *Barrie Examiner*. He wrote that he's "tired," but that it "won't do to just lay about. One must stay active."

I try to think about why.

I think about the telegram carrier coming up the walk—coming up my walk—with his terrible errand, an errand that announced the destruction of the future to the woman who opened the door on that May morning in 1942. Her garden would just have been coming up, the irises and early tulips. I know more about what happened to him on that day than she did. His own mother, opening the door—*that door*—the door that I unlock and open every morning, that I close and lock every night. In a single exhale,

in a telegram.

it all falls down.

It stretches my mind beyond its boundaries to reflect on this telegram. There is something unapproachable in it. The past for me is as opaque as the future. I can't grasp it. The doorbell rings. The world ends.

P.368412/42/P.4.A.

" May, 1942.

Sir,

I am commanded by the Air Council to express to you
their grave concern on learning from the Casualties Officer
of the Royal Canadian Air Force that your son, Pilot Officer
John Randolph Patton, is missing as the result of air
operations on 1st May, 1942, during which he was flying a
Spitfire aircraft and engaged the enemy over Northern France.
This does not necessarily mean that he is killed or wounded,
and if he is a prisoner of war he should be able to communicate

Jack Patton died in a Supermarine Mark V Spitfire, registration number AD-134, just before 4:00 p.m. on May 1, 1942. He was twenty-five years old. The wing commander whose daughter served me tea reported seeing his aircraft strike the Channel. He did not bail. Perhaps he was killed before his plane hit the water. Or perhaps he could not bail because of his height.

I know this: the weather had been bad. On three separate occasions on May 1, they had been sent up and then brought back because of weather. He had been up all of the early morning and afternoon. The weather cleared and then closed in; cleared and then closed in. He must have been very tired when they finally took off from Gravesend at 3:00 p.m. He must have been.

Very, very tired.

The knowable death defines everything. But what does this clinical achievement, this ability to know his fate precisely, amplify? He becomes a representation of himself through these facts. And the silences and quiet spaces where he was and where he might have been are erased. The hope of encountering him as something else is erased. I'm trying to build a different

1st December, 194?.

Mr. John Patton,
52 William Street,
Barrie, Ontario.

Dear Mr. Patton:

I have learned with deep regret
that your son, Pilot Officer John Randolph
Patton, previously reported missing on
Active Service Overseas is now presumed to
have died on May 1st, 194?. I wish to offer
both you and Mrs. Patton my sincere and
heartfelt sympathy.

It is so unfortunate that a prom-
ising career should be thus terminated and
I would like you to know that his loss is
greatly deplored by all those with whom
your son was serving.

Yours sincerely,

(SGD.) C. A. S.

(C.S. Breadner)
Air Marshal,
Chief of the Air Staff.

AW

archive in the front hallway of John and Jessie Patton's house, but I don't know how to do it. My neighbours call it a shrine. That's how I know I am failing.

The train moves through Allandale. Allandale looks beautiful in the dusk, warm lights behind stained glass, recent renovations, paint jobs, new porches, mowed lawns. It's on the brink of its mandated gentrification, again because of the rail line, this time not for the movement of freight in an industrial society but for the movement of people going to Toronto to sell their labour in the global flows of postwar capitalism. The gentrification is coming, but it's not here yet. House after red-brick house slides past the window. I think about the village it might have been, with its homes huddled together for warmth in winter, a modest beacon set beside the deep fold of Kempenfelt Bay. I think about how he would have watched this little railway village slide by and out of his vision for the last time. I wonder if he had a crashing moment of clarity, the sudden certitude that you would never come back, even though you can't quite contemplate it; even though you can't quite believe it possible. Even as it's sliding by, it stands solid there, feeling eternal, feeling like it will always be the same. Warm lamplight glows behind stained glass. Fleurs-de-lys, geometries, Gothic rosettes.

No bombs can fall on it. No mortar rounds can destroy it. It is already gone.

The copyright holder of the Brotherhood of Locomotive Engineers photo is Simcoe County Archives.

THIS IS NOT
THE END OF THE STORY
The Lasting Promise of Section 35

Ian Waddell

> Rights of the Aboriginal Peoples of Canada
>
> 35. (1) The existing aboriginal and treaty rights of the aboriginal peoples of Canada are hereby recognized and affirmed.
>
> (2) In this Act, "aboriginal peoples of Canada" includes the Indian, Inuit and Métis peoples of Canada.
>
> — Constitution Act, 1982

This is the story, or at least one part of the story, of how section 35 came to be. Like any good story, it has to start somewhere, and it starts with Harry Chingee, chief of the Sekani people, who was showing me how to cast a fly rod, while my friend Jack Woodward was wading in the middle of a fast-flowing river. We were near the town of Mackenzie, in central British Columbia, although it did seem like the North to me at the time. It was summer 1977. Sitting on the grassy river-bank, in a forest clearing down a hill from Harry's log house, I was far from Glasgow, where I was born, and far even from Vancouver, where I had arrived via Toronto and set up a law practice. Jack and I were representing the Sekani band for a Royal Commission hearing, whose purpose I have long since forgotten. What I haven't forgotten is how Harry's people had been displaced from their homes the decade before, when the W.A.C. Bennett Dam was built on the Peace River.

As our catch sizzled in a small pan by the water's edge, a couple of big trucks thundered along the road. "Are they your trucks?" I asked Harry. "Are you kidding?" he replied. "They belong to the logging company, and they come and go as they please." Later, as we relaxed by a crackling fire, I pressed him again. Harry, who just passed away two years ago, was a quiet man, but after a long pause he replied, "Ian, I can't stop those damn trucks. I don't have that kind of power." I asked what he would ask for if he were to have some say over the loggers. He told me his people just wanted to be recognized and included, to have a "piece of the action," by which he meant having a say in the place and having their historic land rights recognized.

Later that week, after we'd left Harry's place, Jack and I flew in a small plane over Williston Lake, the vast reservoir behind the hydroelectric dam. Our pilot mentioned how many of the trees had been left standing in the river valley before the flooding, ironic considering all those logging trucks. BC Hydro had said there was no market for the wood, and, besides, it was in a hurry. But now those trees would sometimes rise up from the floor of the lake, shooting to the surface like ballistic missiles. Occasionally, they hit Sekani canoes, holing or capsizing them. Other times, canoes would get caught in a tangle of debris. People had died in both ways.

I was a young, earnest lawyer at the time, and I thought I was familiar with Aboriginal rights. I had read the landmark *Calder* case. I had even spent three years with Tom Berger, the future judge who argued that case, as his assistant on the historic inquiry into a proposed pipeline through the Mackenzie Valley. But I was discovering that I still had a lot to learn.

Maybe the story actually starts in the late 1950s, in a small law firm in North Vancouver. The office belonged to Tom Hurley, a flamboyant and heavy-drinking criminal lawyer. His wife and secretary was Maisie Hurley, an immigrant from England who had founded a newspaper with Indigenous women, the *Native Voice*. One day, Tom returned from lunch with his studious (and sober) law student, Tom Berger, and chided Maisie for accepting an "Indian law case." She walked with the aid of a stick, and when she heard those words, she banged it on the desk: "They own this land. They never gave it up. The Royal Proclamation of 1763!"

After her husband died, Maisie Hurley asked Berger to take another "Indian law case." Two First Nations men from the Nanaimo area, Clifford White and David Bob, had been charged with having six deer carcasses during closed season, contrary to the provisions of the Game Act. Berger argued they had a right under the treaties signed by James Douglas, British Columbia's first governor. That argument wasn't going anywhere with the magistrate, so Berger then raised the Royal Proclamation—for the first time in any court. No luck. But a reporter for the *Province* picked up the idea: LAWYER CLAIMS INDIANS OWN PROVINCE, the headline read.

Berger received plenty of negative calls, and then he heard from Chief Frank Calder, who said the Nisga'a had been trying to argue the same thing for over a century. Berger took their case, *Calder et al. v. Attorney-General of British Columbia,* all the way to the Supreme Court of Canada. In 1973, the court ruled that Aboriginal title had indeed existed when George III issued the Royal Proclamation centuries before. That decision was the first time the Canadian legal system acknowledged the existence of Aboriginal title and that such title existed independent of colonial law. The court was split, however, on whether the Nisga'a claim was valid. Three judges ruled that while Aboriginal title may have existed at one point, it had since been extinguished. Three other judges affirmed Nisga'a title, arguing that it had never been extinguished through treaty or statute. The seventh judge dismissed the case on a technicality. The federal justice minister, John Turner, was so impressed by Berger's legal skills that he appointed him to the Supreme Court of British Columbia.

We could probably start this story another way entirely. In the early 1970s, I was the head of the Storefront Lawyers in Vancouver when I began working with Berger, by this time a judge, on a unified family court project. Not long after that, Pierre Elliott Trudeau, who had a minority government dependent on the support of David Lewis, appointed Berger (a former NDP Member of Parliament and BC party leader) to head a Royal Commission on the proposed Mackenzie Valley Pipeline, which would carry Alaskan and Canadian delta gas south. It was to be the largest private construction project in history. Berger hired me as his assistant.

The Berger Inquiry was officially launched by an order-in-council on March 21, 1974. It was Berger's idea to hold the bulk of the hearings away from Ottawa, a major departure from the way public inquiries were usually run at the time. "I want the people who live in the North, who make the North their home, to tell me in their own language and in their own way what they would say to the government of Canada," he said. One hearing, in Old Crow, Yukon, lasted almost a week; we listened to the whole town.

Because the hearings were held far from the country's population centres, extensive media coverage was crucial. CBC North broadcast every night in six languages, and the journalist Martin O'Malley brought the events to *Globe and Mail* readers almost every day. The inquiry was shown regularly on the national news. In fact, no previous inquiry had been broadcast the way this one was (and only the Truth and Reconciliation Commission has had such coverage since). Canadians began to notice.

The process helped develop a whole generation of Indigenous leaders. Nellie Cournoyea, from Inuvik, worked with the

Committee for Original People's Entitlement, which represented the Inuit. She would become the sixth premier of the Northwest Territories, and later chaired the Aboriginal Pipeline Group and the Inuvialuit Regional Corporation. Frank T'Seleie was a young Dene chief who publicly challenged Bob Blair of Foothills Pipe Lines. He said he would put his body in front of the construction equipment. After land claims were settled, T'Seleie became a proponent of the pipeline, which then included Indigenous partners. The boyish Stephen Kakfwi helped organize the Dene's presentations to Berger. He became president of the Dene Nation and the ninth premier of the Northwest Territories. Dave Porter, who used to carry equipment for CBC crews, was elected to the Yukon Legislative Assembly and went on to be executive director of the Yukon Human Rights Commission and a negotiator for the Kaska Dena Council. Jim Antoine, then the quiet but charismatic twenty-six-year-old chief of the Fort Simpson Dene, greeted John Paul II on the 1987 papal visit and also became a premier of the Northwest Territories. And Georges Erasmus cut his teeth at the inquiry, appearing for the Dene Nation (called the Indian Brotherhood at the time). He became national chief of the Assembly of First Nations and co-chaired the Royal Commission on Aboriginal Peoples.

After the Berger Inquiry ended in April 1977, I returned to practising law in Vancouver, which led me to that Sekani client and the opportunity to fish with Harry Chingee. Before we left town, Harry took Jack Woodward and me, along with Jim Fulton, a local probation officer, and his wife, Liz, up a bumpy logging road to the top of Morfee Mountain. At the summit, a small group of Sekani were having a late afternoon picnic. I recognized some of them from the Berger hearings, including a good friend of Harry's, who seemed like a sort of spiritual leader. As we watched the sunset, Jim and I confessed that we were going to try to win the federal NDP nominations in Skeena (for Jim) and in Vancouver Kingsway (for me). Both would be tough fights, and we knew it would be even tougher to knock off the incumbents in the general election that would have to be called sometime in 1979. Harry's friend told us that we were both going to win. Everyone cheered, and we did a little dance holding hands (it was the '70s, after all).

Harry's friend was right: Jim and I won upset victories in the May 1979 general election, which produced a minority government that lasted to December, under Joe Clark. In February 1980, Trudeau rose from the dead and formed a majority government—but with only two of the seventy-five seats that represented the four Western provinces. (The Liberals didn't have a seat west of Lloyd Axworthy's in Winnipeg.) Fulton and I were re-elected.

In the run-up to the 1980 Quebec referendum, the Parti Québécois premier, René Lévesque, led the separatists, while Trudeau led the federalist side. Canada was lucky to have him there. (Joe Clark, when he was prime minister, had decided to leave the fight to the province's Opposition leader, Claude Ryan.) It's impossible to predict what might have happened without federal involvement, but Trudeau and others campaigned actively against separation, and on May 20, three months after the Liberals had regained power, the No side, against sovereignty, won by 59.56 percent.

Before the vote, in a speech in Montreal, Trudeau stated that the referendum showed the need for change, and he pledged he would work with the premiers to "renew" Canada's constitution. He knew that he'd have more influence in any constitutional discussion if his cabinet included representation from the West. To this end, he was in talks with Ed Broadbent about tapping some NDP MPs as ministers. Broadbent ultimately rejected the idea but indicated he would support Trudeau's constitutional package. Unknown to Trudeau or the public, this produced what amounted to a revolt inside the NDP caucus.

A constitution is the fundamental law of any country—the rules by which it governs itself. In 1980, Canada's constitution was essentially the British North America Act of 1867. Any significant changes had to be made by the Parliament of the United Kingdom on the advice of Canada. After numerous meetings with the premiers, and numerous tentative agreements that failed when provinces backed out or refused to support him, Trudeau rather courageously presented his constitutional package, which included a Charter of Rights and Freedoms and the promise of a national referendum on the amending formula, on October 6, 1980. It's hard to overstate the intensity of the debate that followed. At one point, the British high commissioner, Sir John Ford, even got kicked out of Canada for suggesting things might not get past Westminster.

Trudeau soon found that only two provinces, Ontario and New Brunswick, supported his plan. The others—the so-called Gang of Eight—were vehemently against it. Quebec wanted a veto on any constitutional amendment; Saskatchewan and Manitoba were against a court-interpreted Charter; Alberta, Newfoundland, and Saskatchewan wanted provincial resource control embedded in the constitution; and so on. Within the NDP caucus, Pauline Jewett and Margaret Mitchell wanted to see language around women's rights. Svend Robinson wanted the Charter strengthened generally. Lorne Nystrom and Simon De Jong wanted Saskatchewan's concerns addressed. And Jim Manly, Jim Fulton, and I wanted Aboriginal rights included.

Of course, the story really begins long, long ago, with the tragedies and injustices that Indigenous peoples have faced on this land for centuries. I began to appreciate this part of the story as a young criminal lawyer in Vancouver, working near Hastings and Main. And as counsel to Tom Berger during the Mackenzie Valley Pipeline Inquiry, I started to see how First Nations could regain real political and economic power within the modern Canadian framework through the formal recognition of their rights. The scope of those rights became clear to me during Berger's countless meetings, from Old Crow to Fort Smith, as people spoke of their love of the land and their use of that land for hunting and fishing since time immemorial. They had never surrendered title, even as they had lost access to those lands and the resources that went with them.

In the latter part of 1980, the constitutional debate was taking place in joint hearings before the Senate and the House of Commons. Jack Woodward had appeared there as counsel for the loquacious and determined George Watts, chief of the Nuu-chah-nulth Tribal Council, who was arguing for a clause that would protect Aboriginal rights. Years before, in 1969, Pierre Trudeau had called those rights "historical might-have-beens." To his credit, Trudeau changed his mind over the course of the debate. This may have been because he needed the NDP's backing for his constitutional package. Whatever the reason, he sent his loyal lieutenant and justice minister, Jean Chrétien, to negotiate our support. That is why I found myself in Broadbent's office—653C—a few days later. As chance would have it, Don Rosenbloom, who was counsel with Berger in the *Calder* case, was in Ottawa; I asked him to join me, Ed, and Marc Eliesen, Broadbent's chief of research, to help negotiate a deal. Woodward happened to be back in Ottawa, and I put him to work as well.

Eliesen concentrated on drafting the amendment that clarified provincial control of resources (now section 92A of the Constitution Act, 1867). This would help bring Saskatchewan and Alberta on board. Jack, Don, and I concentrated on the Aboriginal rights amendment. Chrétien was at first reluctant. "I have to report to the boss, you know," he said as the sun began to set over the Ottawa River. But with the help of some freshly brewed coffee, he hung in there. We discussed the issue and its potential ramifications. (I also knew that he was under intense pressure from Indigenous groups, who were literally camped in offices, buildings, and tents around downtown Ottawa.)

A vote was called in the House on another matter, so we took a break from the negotiations. I scurried back to my office, in the Confederation Building, to find Woodward at the typewriter drafting a clause. He was the only one of us who knew how to type. I took his draft back to Rosenbloom. Don and I thought the wording was too general, so Don went next door to Ed's secretary's office and called Vancouver. He talked to Tom Berger and Jim Aldridge and came back saying that Berger, in particular, had advised us to keep the wording general. This would give the courts space to develop the law. We took Jack's draft and tweaked it a bit more—made it simpler, really. And we gave this to Chrétien.

The next day, Chrétien took the clause to the joint parliamentary committee, co-chaired by Serge Joyal and Harry Hays. Harry Daniels, president of the Métis National Council and the Native Council of Canada, had been attending the hearings. He grabbed Chrétien by the lapels as he was going into the meeting and told him not to forget the Métis people. Svend Robinson, who was standing nearby, quickly scribbled down a definition: "Aboriginals include Indian, Inuit, and Métis." (I have always thought that if there is a heaven, a prominent place should be reserved there for Harry. I suspect Svend doesn't believe in heaven, but if he does end up there, he should get a prominent place too.)

Ultimately, the House of Commons passed the draft constitutional agreement in February 1981, but several provinces challenged Trudeau's plan to unilaterally patriate the constitution. That September, the Supreme Court ruled that such an act might be legal, but that it violated existing constitutional conventions. So the prime minister was forced to go back to the premiers one more time. Finally, on November 5, 1981, Ottawa reached a deal with the provinces—all except Quebec. In the process, the clauses that had entrenched Aboriginal and treaty rights, as well as women's equality rights, in the new constitution were somehow removed.

Tom Berger responded to the removal of Aboriginal rights from the agreement in an op-ed for the *Globe and Mail* and in a speech he delivered in Guelph, Ontario:

> No words can deny what happened. The first Canadians—a million people and more—have had their answer from Canada's statesmen. They cannot look to any of our governments to defend the idea that they are entitled to a distinct and contemporary place in Canadian life. Under the new constitution the first Canadians shall be the last. This is not the end of the story. The native peoples have not come this far to turn back now.

Because they must appear impartial, judges are not supposed to speak on political matters. But should a judge remain silent if, by instead speaking out, he may prevent a great injustice to a minority?

Berger put his judicial career on the line, and he was rebuked by Trudeau (who eventually backtracked). A conservative judge complained to the Canadian Judicial Council, which cited Berger for an "indiscretion." In the end, Berger resigned. He spoke out, and he paid the price. It probably cost him a future appointment to the Supreme Court, which was a great loss for Canada. But that's what civil disobedience is all about. His unique voice made a difference in the constitutional debate, especially his advice to keep the clause general so it could grow legally.

If the Judicial Council had tried to impeach Berger, or if the government had failed to restore Aboriginal rights, I believe Broadbent and our NDP caucus would have withdrawn our support for Trudeau's package altogether, which would have tied the House of Commons in knots. As it was, Indigenous leaders and allies, including the Vancouver lawyer Louise Mandell and hundreds of others, flocked to Ottawa by train, aboard the Constitution Express. They forced the prime minister and the premiers to restore section 35. The word *existing* was added to placate some premiers, but that had little effect. In fact, courts have subsequently said that it actually reinforces the phrase "recognized and affirmed."

As I look back on the negotiations, I think of the moral courage of Ed Broadbent, who had to step back from his original approval of the package and face the prime minister's anger. I think of Tom Berger, who put his judicial robes on the line. And I think of Pierre Trudeau himself, who had the intellectual courage to listen and change his mind. George Watts, Jack Woodward, Don Rosenbloom, Jim Aldridge, and Jean Chrétien—they all worked tirelessly. Above all, I think of the steadfastness of Indigenous people throughout Canada, with their leaders and their voices and their drums in all those villages and fish camps. They beat away our fatigue.

I've tried to tell this story before, including in my 2018 memoir, *Take the Torch*. And maybe the right place to start all along would have been with Ronald Sparrow, a fisherman, who just passed away in September. Back in 1984, shortly before he turned forty, Bud was arrested on the Fraser River and charged with violating his Coast Salish band's fishing licence. But the charge, he argued, violated his rights.

Six years later, in 1990, the Supreme Court of Canada agreed with him. In their landmark opinion, the chief justice, Brian Dickson, and Gérard La Forest held that section 35 should be given a generous, liberal interpretation: "It is clear, then, that s. 35 (1) of the *Constitution Act, 1982,* represents the culmination of a long and difficult struggle in both the political forum and the courts for the constitutional recognition of aboriginal rights." The so-called Sparrow test was born.

It's now been thirty years since Bud's case was decided and almost forty years since the passage of the Constitution Act of 1982. Section 35 has been cited in over 350 other decisions. In *Delgamuukw v. British Columbia,* for example, brought by the Wet'suwet'en hereditary chiefs and the Gitxsan nation, the Supreme Court held that Aboriginal title still existed in the unceded territories and would have to be settled. The justices basically said: government, get on with it. Then, under the leadership of Beverley McLachlin, from 2000 to 2017, the court gave further life to the clause, emphasizing that the duty to consult is grounded in the principle of the Crown's honour—that its purpose is reconciliation between Ottawa and Indigenous peoples.

Section 35 is a living clause that has revolutionized the relationship between Indigenous peoples and the Canadian state—one that has moved from statute-based laws and old treaties to recognized land claims to enshrined constitutional rights. The courts, to their great credit, have done their part. Now is the time for the politicians. True reconciliation will require further changes in that relationship. The tools are all out there.

Today, we need the political will and perhaps a modern Royal Proclamation—one that will formally recognize Indigenous people as a founding nation of Canada and that will lay out a road map to a workable third level of government. But that is another story altogether, one yet to be written.

THE FUTURE ACCIDENTAL

Rob Winger

> Poetry has that ability to reconstitute language; it uses
> time. It can make you see the xylem between the then and
> the after, or the now and the after. It has no obligation to
> the present. It *is* time.
>
> — Dionne Brand

At a tiny farm-to-table restaurant on Ossington Avenue, I
lean over my cherry flan. It's the end of the meal. I've already
eaten most of my whipped cream. Across from me, my friend
remains phoneless and much smarter than I'll ever be. She
insists not on a personal resistance to technology but instead
on a refusal to be dictated by it. "I'll be out to dinner with
eight friends," she says, "and fully half will be looking down,
like this." Under the table, she holds her palm flat and stares
at it. And she clarifies: it's not *affect* but *effect*—the way our
lives adjust to technology until that technology reshapes how
we organize our lives. The way, at Angkor Wat one morning
five years ago, she says, each person around her privileged
the machines in their pockets, not the ones behind tissue and
bone, holding up their screens between their faces and each
relief sculpture lit by the vital, irreplaceable Siem Reap dawn.

ROB WINGER

Susan Sontag seems already to have understood this almost forty years ago. In *On Photography,* she postulates that then-contemporary 1970s tourist picture taking is really an extension of capital, an activity that allows those ensnared in the economies of market exploitation to rationalize the utility of a break from the grind without feeling too bad about taking a holiday. My friend and I both know this. Either one of us might quote Georg Simmel's 1903 essay "The Metropolis and Mental Life," which claims that modern urban reality allows for both a sense of "personal freedom" and a simultaneous suspicion that each of us is just "a mere cog in an enormous organization of things and powers." Or we might recall a seemingly opposite impulse from the same era: John Muir, treed in his nineteenth-century California redwoods, glorying in the salve of electricity-free natural spaces. Both postures, it seems to me, reflect a historically consistent way of being in the world that many of us tend to misread as uniquely, grotesquely present tense.

"I'm always suspicious," I say, our dessert nearly done, "of the idea that anything is really new."

Right now, almost all of us have phones in our pockets. So almost all of us carry a full library that's accessible with a search bar and the means to access and pay a cellular bill; there, on our pocketed screens, is the capacity to produce more images in a single day than could be created in a decade a hundred years ago; there we find satellite access to eons of pixelated maps we now routinely use to navigate new cities or subway lines. Does this mean that the digital age, the social-media age, the present age is in any way fundamentally different from what preceded it? Does the invention of the cellphone and the internet constitute a wholly new kind of human experience, as we're so often told it does? And what do we mean when we say the word *new* anyhow?

In almost any decade within the past two centuries, after all, one can almost always, with accuracy, make these sorts of statements: the human race has never gone as fast as it's going now; we've never wrecked so much so quickly; we've never created or seen so many images; we've never been closer to living in a single social village; we've never seen such violence; the world has never been so small. In his easy 1850s New England cabin, Henry David Thoreau seemed to confirm this sort of present-tense exceptionalism. He famously dismissed daily newspaper reportage by claiming, in *Walden,* both that "To a philosopher, all *news,* as it is called, is gossip" and that he "could easily do without the post-office"; both statements react to the invasion by the 1840s of daily newspapers into everyday American life. To Thoreau, newspaper news simply increased the volume, traffic, and scale of all the junk already circulating.

"So," my friend says across the table, "maybe the question is about urgency, not singularity." Maybe when we say "new" we're talking about energy, not a collapsing or dividing of history into tidy eras such as The Past and The Present. Maybe we're talking about a feeling or a condition, not an era or an absolute.

Purists like Thoreau were supposedly appalled with people in mid-century cafés placing between themselves and their companions giant sheaves of newsprint, thereby allowing technology—since even a paper or a book is a form of technology—to interrupt otherwise engaged, face-to-face exchanges. While different in speed and volume than contemporary digital sources, nineteenth-century newspapers were anchored by an algorithmic market economy—they only stayed in business by successfully targeting ads to their audiences. To me, Thoreau's critiques sound a whole lot like what Cal Newport calls the vital need for "digital minimalism," which advises us to save ourselves from dopamine-releasing clickbait addictions, fears of missing out, or nagging urges to frame and regulate our lives online. That urge to check, post, and update also echoes the way Sontag's tourists documented their hikes to the edge of the Grand Canyon: both tasks can feel like work rather than play.

What then, if anything, marks our time, here and now, as unique? And is the implicit quest for novelty even the right thing to be thinking about? Does any urge to say our time is different or more complex than the supposedly "simpler" times that came before reveal a narrowness similar to the egotistical branding demanded by most social-media platforms? And, if so, what does this say about my own attempts to focus on what's new? Is Thoreau really right that the only news is the kind that lasts?

Here are some lines written by one of my literary heroes, American poet Adrienne Rich, way back in the early 1990s, nearly thirty years ago—lines I read on a commuter train on my way to see my friend at this table where we're now sitting—that conclude the horror-filled, beautiful title sequence of her book *An Atlas of the Difficult World*:

> I know you are reading this poem listening for
>   something, torn
>   between bitterness and hope
> turning back once again to the task you
>   cannot refuse.
> I know you are reading this poem because
>   there is nothing else
>   left to read
> there where you have landed, stripped
>   as you are.

How is it possible that such lines remain fully contemporary? How is it possible for Rich's decades-old stanzas to speak so precisely about all the seemingly new versions of populism rising around the world right now? The answer, I think, cannot simply involve myths of genius or artistic immortality. As

Rich's American contemporary Kurt Vonnegut noted, promoting such familiar tropes would probably just be "show business."

The answer, instead, seems to involve establishing situation and context, then sharing with sureness any possible faith in provisional knowledge; that's what happens, for me, in the best moments of the best kinds of reading or writing. In our current era—as long as what we say is not extremist, hateful, fundamentalist, ill-informed, or functionally closed—to declare anything with certainty is a revolutionary act. It is no longer rebellious or novel to point out all the tiny ways in which what we think we know cannot possibly be absolute. Instead, it's a revolution to locate with poetic precision, as Rich so often does, one boat on one sea, one wreck accessed by one ladder that leads down into a single, singular ocean. It's a revolution to declare we know any answers.

All of us who are at least partially awake to the state of the twenty-first-century world recognize the ebb and flow that Rich locates in the lines above: we're "torn," she writes, "between bitterness and hope." And, sadly, this is not news, especially given the ways that the ugliest parts of populism continue to shape the cultural realities of so many who can't claim the privileged qualifiers I was able, for so long, to ignore: middle-class, cishet, white, male. Perhaps binaries such as "bitterness and hope," as I read them, are therefore foundational; they certainly feel like primary elements in Ecclesiastes or the Tao Te Ching or the Dhammapada. What's *new*, maybe, in the sense Thoreau might have meant it, is the constant newness reactivated when we read lines that cheat or complicate time, that clarify our present conditions without any need for definitive historical footnotes. What's new is our apprehension, over and over, of lines floated forward to us as so many proverbial bottled messages.

When I uncork a line in a novel or poem that accomplishes this sense of revolutionary newness—a newness that risks saying it might know, despite all the evidence that reminds us that we can't quite know— I react less with my scholarly training or aesthetic judgment than I do with my body. I react involuntarily. When I read such lines, such as the immaculate conclusion to Toni Morrison's novel *Song of Solomon,* or the final stanzas of Pablo Neruda's "Ode to the Onion," or the best poems of Adrienne Rich, this is what happens: the hairs on my arms and on the back of my neck stand on end, my body shivers, there's a drop in my stomach as though I'm descending a small hill at top speed in a car on a country road, my eyes well up, my throat swells and chokes, I can't speak. Something breaks and is healed all at once.

The way I respond to the world is informed by my knowledge of this place, which simultaneously allows for an intuitive bodily reaction and an intellectual recognition of declaration as revolutionary risk. Is this response influenced by technological newness, or by the ways we might be shaped by social media, or by the necessity to accelerate into digital all the processes so many of us first learned in analog? Does it make any sense to mourn the loss of the latency between exposing a negative image on film and witnessing its positive results on paper? I'm thinking about these questions at the table, where my friend still holds her palm flat, trying to understand what's new, if anything, in how all of us are formulating and engaging with and disconnecting from the worlds around us.

Those of us who read and write poetry—regardless of whether it's performative or conceptual or lyrical and on the page—are answering these questions when we use language that doesn't pretend, that rejects the fashionable or polite, that declares the weird truths it sees. And such truths can't be simplified into any sort of slogan, wherein sure declaration equals new knowledge equals safe beauty. Rather than simply adopting Ezra Pound's old "make it new" mantra—advice so often twisted in the past century into formulations that translate as "make it *look* new" or "make it *seem* new"—such declarations perhaps involve responding with both artistic integrity and ethical honesty to whatever we find around us.

Moral and political responses to the awful public hatefulness of right-wing populism are required not only in poetry, of course, but also in real-life conversations and contexts. The left, for all its excellent intentions, tends to imitate the machinations of the right on social media, speaking directly to its own constituents in its own language to villainize and dehumanize its own targets. That I agree with the moral assumptions of those who engage in such targeting is troubling to me. But I worry that something like writing a poem is a similar retreat, a movement back into silo thinking, into choir-preaching, into the ease of beauty. Is Phyllis Webb still right, then, that "the proper response to a poem is another poem"?

To think about this question, I'm trying to understand the urgencies of the now without simply dividing history into a tidy before-and-after, a misleading this-and-only-this. I'm testing what might be new in what we like to call "our time." Are the ways we pose for a coiffed selfie essentially any different than the ways we've always put on fashionable masks to enact public versions of ourselves? And can't an insistence on truth-telling also be a game, a ruse, a limitation, a humblebrag? Has our era's demand always to respond, always like, always showcase our daily lives truly reshaped how we apprehend, understand, and translate the world? I'm unsure. It seems possible that the digital networks we invented to extend our analog lives are moving toward replacing them instead. It seems plausible that the chemistry we keep leaching into the air and water may alter us biologically. It seems probable that our attention is divided. But I also recognize the presentism that informs such common proclamations. Is the presentist belief that things are so much worse than they were before (or, if you really dig texting or modern dentistry, so much better) just a symptom of the narcissism supposedly fuelling contemporary culture? And if it is, then what to think about something irrefutably present tense, like climate change?

Thinking about writing poetry today, regardless of any answers to such queries, necessitates at least a recognition of the potentially shifting parameters of the world that will receive it (if we intend to write for anyone other than ourselves, that is). Self-awareness and honesty might be the original twin poles necessary for magnetizing the poetic globe, but how do we locate ourselves now, with so many parts of the world still on fire, so many of us still locked up, so many still rolling in gold coins? Part of the answer surely has to do with the individuation and situated knowledge necessary for using words such as *I* or *we* or *you*: who do these exclude or accuse?

Again, Adrienne Rich always seems to offer me the best answers to such questions, this time in her 1984 essay "Notes toward a Politics of Location":

> *The difficulty of saying I*—a phrase from the East German novelist Christa Wolf. But once having said it, as we realize the necessity to go further, isn't there a difficulty of saying "we"? *You cannot speak for me. I cannot speak for us.* Two thoughts: there is no liberation that only knows how to say "I"; there is no collective movement that speaks for each of us all the way through.

Like Milkman Dead rising above the last page of *Song of Solomon* or the slices performed at the end of "Ode to the Onion," these lines provoke the necessary breakage that locates me in the world, now. They both limit and open who is included in saying *I* or *we* or *you*. They tell us, thirty-five years after they're written, what poetic truth can offer: a way to locate ourselves—in history, in culture, in geography, in our own bodies, in our own time—that's not necessarily the present or the past or the future, but more what I'd tentatively like to call the future accidental. I mean for this phrase, *the future accidental,* to function as both a categorical label (the nature of the dynamic I'm sketching) and as a verb tense (the grammatical mode within which that dynamic is expressed).

Used as both label and verb tense, the term implies at least two primary thoughts. First, it implies the obvious idea of chance (minus all notions of astrological destiny, I admit): the textual "accident" that might place a certain book or poem in your life at a certain time, a placement that fuses two types of present tense in the moment of reception—the now of the writer's act of writing and the now of the reader's act of reading. That this action is always new signals the complete cycle, wherein the latent newness of what's recorded is only developed in the newness of reception—so a poem's future comprises both its past circulation and recording and, simultaneously, the eventual newness of our eyes on its lines. Second, the term implies "accidental" in the musical sense, wherein the flats, sharps, and naturals that occur when playing or listening to music signal moments within a system that don't quite obey that system's most common expectations, moments that obscure or shift the expected notes in any declared scale, signalling that what's happening, at any given moment, sometimes concerns the pauses or exclusions between expected notes. Thus, I mean "accidental" to signal the minor notes within and against recognizably major systems, notes that demarcate what doesn't quite fit into normalcy or reason. That quiet refutation of system, recorded in the poem, left dormant in the shelved book, is made new each time it's activated by a reader who's awake, who also activates their own accidentals.

What's new in the future accidental—since it marks not just newness but renewal, reinvention, translation—is always new. What's novel is terminal. While the way forward often requires a consideration of the way back—the conditions that continue to form and inform us—what seems more essential in the future accidental is perhaps the way *inward,* where we might best understand ourselves by being humble, locating our moments as functionally similar to those that come before us, yet urgently individual, privately revolutionary, and particular. Our own present tense is not wider, faster, more complex, more urgent than any other one we've seen. But it's helpful to admit that what I see as new—as now— still remains more immediate to me, here, at the table we're sharing, than the ways I might look into other mirrors, or atlases, or histories; that sense of the new as now is what we have between us.

Two thoughts, then, might make some sense here: the first is from Jeanette Winterson's wondrous first novel, *Oranges Are Not the Only Fruit*; the second appears in her equally magical book *Sexing the Cherry*, a statement that is part of a list of widely accepted "Lies":

1. "But not all dark places need light, I have to remember that."
2. Lie: "The difference between the past and the future is that one has happened while the other has not."

I still think, despite the education I've been lucky enough to get, that I—and perhaps many of us?—remain addicted to the simplicities of binary thinking, of this versus that, too happy to solve half empty with half full, especially since simplistically looking on the bright side so often causes blindness rather than clarity. A partial answer to what's new might involve, therefore, not an either/or but a both/and, a recognition of simultaneity. The danger, there, is replacing binary thinking with a new sort of fundamentalism, a new way to finalize and answer questions that might be more valuable as provocations or organizing principles than as multiple-choice queries. We can't solve binary thinking by simply disallowing binary thinking, in other words—such a solution would be a double negative. Darkness and light, then, might have to coexist; past and future may always involve each other. Or, as Michel-Rolph Trouillot puts it in *Silencing the Past,* "Time here is not mere chronological continuity. It is the range of disjointed moments, practices, and symbols that thread the historical relations between events and narrative."

Maybe this is why, when considering what's new, I sometimes imagine a certain kind of nineteenth-century life. In the space of one lifetime, electric light was invented and flooded city streets and buildings, photography was created and became commonplace, certain forms of legal slavery were made officially illegal, and cables were placed in the Atlantic to carry signals that used to require a three-week packet-ship crossing. But have the primary structures that inspired good old Ned Ludd to smash his 1770s stocking frames really shifted in what we tend to call "our time"? Does the swiftness of contemporary brutality or the extraction of limited resources that currently fuel our Western privileges—coltan now, not ivory—constitute any real, systemic, distributive change from the economies that precede this one? If anything has become new in our own time, perhaps it's the details of the design, not the drawing table itself. So how can we best think about the present, unprecedented portability and ubiquity of the trends that locate us after the end of that imagined nineteenth-century life?

Here's a possible answer: my friend's palm, still under the table, still flat. Here's my beer glass, already empty. Here's the sun, just so, finding all the things we've shared here, now, new, between us. And even that newness isn't new; even this now has its own exacting histories.

It's only in such moments of clear sight—like reading or writing what feels like the right lines so that my body overtakes my mind and the whole Cartesian balancing act fuses into a singular, non-binary vision fuelled by shared language—that I'm able both to detect the monsters we're always sketching at the edges of our own little oceans and to navigate past the shore into the already inhabited mainland, hair standing on end. That's not news. It's now. And now can happen any time.

ON LEAVING AND ON GOING BACK

Women Walking

Jenna Butler and *Yvonne Blomer*

> *There she goes, (there she goes again) / Racing through my*
> *brain / And I just can't contain / This feeling that remains*
> ... as sung by Sixpence None the Richer

We travel to Assisi, Italy, and stay for two weeks, then train on to Venice, as writers, women, friends. In our hands, we hold an almost unbelievable opportunity to spend two full weeks walking and working, to live fully as writers supported by a residency, a grant, and the much-loved family and community members who hold our spaces at home for us. As women writing and walking together, we strive to wrap our heads around this sudden freedom, this opportunity. As we walk, we speak our way deeper into questions of writing and voice, of belonging and place, of freedom and family. As women in the world, we ponder our stay here at a time when any kind of air travel also compromises our planet. There are no easy answers. There is only the two of us, measuring with our strides the back roads and shady stairways of an ancient city, the breadth of our questions on the page.

1.

How to preserve this: solitude,
work, wildness. The heart.

The heart too is wild. Night's coming
changes light. Day coming.

What is resumed in daylight,
the homeward journey. What roles.

Centre's stone; story's root. I tell you,
this thread too is our own.

All the stories we hold in this world.
Carrying multitudes is a kind of home.

2. Yvonne

On our second night in Assisi, Jenna and I walk the narrow brick streets, we meander up and left and down and right, gradually getting to know the paths, arches, and shopfronts at the centre of Assisi. Over the next two weeks, we will venture farther and farther and at later and later hours. We will become recognizable to the residents.

We climb a low set of stairs, turn, and, lit by a lantern, see a trailing jasmine plant on the outside wall of an intertwined, connected, rebuilt building. Jenna picks a flower and holds it to her nose. "Whoops, Brian," I say to her, and we laugh and fall into a discussion of a *Tyee* article by Brian Brett we'd both read before leaving our homes in Canada. In the article, Brett talks about his cancer diagnosis and his addiction to picking, and even pruning, boulevard flowers in Vancouver.

"Whoops, Brian" becomes one of our mantras. Jenna cannot keep her fingers off flowers, her nose out of them. We wander darkened laneways that first night, just getting a feel for what will become a habit of night-walking the lit, peopled streets of Assisi. We throw Brian Brett's lines back and forth as we walk, relieved to learn that his cancer is not terminal, and that he's curbing his addiction to pruning city flowers. Jenna's may be just blooming.

3. Jenna

We are both opening and stretching to meet the kind of walking Assisi requires of us. For the first few days, Yvonne and I are in minor agony: calves aching, legs straining up and down the many flights of stairs that form the spine of this walled city. But just as the city's frame causes us this daily hurt, it also asks of us something quite marvellous: to set aside the fear we hold as women and to go out exploring. The light draws us out, rich and deep across the old rose stone, and the crowds, boisterous and joyful, pull us first to our window and then out onto the narrow streets. Over the weeks, just as our bodies strengthen to meet the constant inclines of the city, our world opens too: onto the sunlit terraces and patios, the shadowy church vestibules and grape-shaded arbours of Assisi.

My sense of way-finding has always been closely connected to plants, and as the city unfurls its back streets and hidden alleyways to us, plants become my way of navigating space. This proves a source of endless amusement to Yvonne: I can't keep my hands off the olive leaves, their crisp silver rattle, or the sweet jasmine, the July-brittle roses. Not always plucking, but touching—I walk with a hand outstretched to the walled gardens as we navigate the city.

The light, the gardens, the draw of the crowds, and our ever-changing, adapting bodies—day after day, we are pulled by this place to explore, to stretch ourselves in ways we wouldn't have dared back home, women walking. Our biggest shift is the change to walking at night: in July's fever pitch of heat, the days are almost too hot to bear, and so we venture out after sundown to quiet cafés for supper, and from there into the empty back roads of the city. Bounded by the walls, enlivened by the evening scents of jasmine and gardenia, these back roads offer us a chance to navigate deep into the city by night. As women, we go cautiously, all senses engaged, but it's the very permission of it—the heat-hazed, languid evenings, the nearby presence of crowds in the cafés on the square—that entreats us to try this new way of walking.

4. Yvonne

I recall the pinch of tight calf muscles from the low steps and steep hills. The bell towers, the church bells, the darkened basilica, and my sudden desire, no, need, to take rubbings of stone shapes, of markings, and of lightly sculptured building sides. This too, like night walking, is a way to absorb Assisi. To touch and connect and have a sensory way of taking the scent and talc dryness of stone into my fingers and nose. We purchase pastels in a bookstore that has been running for nearly two hundred years. I cut squares and rectangles from our white waxy paper shopping bags, smooth them flat, and every day carry this rubbing kit in my backpack. Jenna plays lookout while I creep up close to a window frame, a wall, a door, a sculpture to rub my black or golden crayon over the awkwardly held paper.

As I ponder some of these moments, my heart sings with a sense of freedom, though I am uneasy with a word like *freedom*. Yet I'm going to use it here. *Release* fits too, though as we settle more and more comfortably into the margin of our lives in this space, I begin to fill up, to fill the space. Begin to stop sleeping, too eager to be present for every moment. We walk into the late hours, talk past midnight, sip limoncello, then sit up writing in our separate rooms.

It is a strain—the pull of the writing life—a strain to be pulled from it. But also, to be pulled towards and away by equal forces: child, husband, life. I long to keep on the path and walk and walk until the view is clear and the sentences whole. So many ways to understand the desire paths that web out and braid in, as women and as walkers. I realize the innumerable measures and judgments society places on women that box and constrain us. In judgment, in analysis, in warning, with ideas of beauty and strength, and defined roles. In these clear, bright-lit days, walking and late night talking with Jenna, I feel a turning away from such restraints and rules. Though I judge myself, in my thoughts, for leaving, for not being good enough, I also try to let myself be the woman I am, who wishes to leave and have time on her own. Time with my work. Who revels in being on a mountain path, solo, and unknown. I revel in the long, late nights with a friend, contemplating life, falling into difficult conversations, stories of our mothers; tears of loss and tears of frustration.

Lauren Elkin explores the possibilities of the female *flâneur,* the *flaneuse.* In her book titled *Flâneuse,* she writes, "Once I began to look for the *flâneuse,* I spotted her everywhere. I caught her standing on street corners in New York and coming through doorways in Kyoto ... She is going somewhere, or coming from somewhere; she is saturated with in-betweenness." This is Jenna and me as we walk the streets of Assisi. We are full of the in-between, while being anchored on the uneven and ancient brick paths.

Eventually, we will have to pack and leave Assisi. We will wend our way to the busier streets of Venice. Packing begins to ready us both for the bigger move home, and the shift from walking and following desire paths to re-entering paths that are already lightly etched on the earth ahead of us.

Pigeons brood outside my bedroom window in Assisi. The view from here is a layered history in rock and brick wall and chimney. I have entered the layers on foot and followed Jenna and the light towards openings in the view—to hilltop and narrow tunnelled route. I look out at this wall, these layered walls, I see something new, and this is a surprise and a lesson in looking and a reminder of why travel, following unique desire paths, is important.

5. Jenna

Yes, I understand the unease with *freedom* as word, as concept. Who really is free? We're all tied in some way to domestic roles, familial expectations, economic drives. Conscience. Perhaps love.

I live in a very wide, vast space back home, and when I come to a place like Assisi, I find myself seeking and creating ritual as a way of defining my momentary life here. Preferred walks. Familiar places to shop and eat and consider the landscape, and to write. Work times and rest times. And I find myself looking for ceremony as a way of deeper grounding and locating: pausing for the space of the noon-hour bells, the quiet evening walk to the great basilica once the heat of the day has faded. How I breathe in certain spaces, how the walls of my body lift out and away, the everyday become part of something larger, more profound. Robin Wall Kimmerer says, "That, I think, is the power of ceremony. It marries the mundane to the sacred. The water turns to wine; the coffee to a prayer." Ceremony as an act of rooting, familiarizing, forming a small home. Walking here, in this place of pilgrimage, becomes the most essential of ceremonies.

And then moving on! That's the dilemma of travel, isn't it? How to keep staying open to all those small homes out there that will come, all the places that take a part of you and leave something changed, charged, in their wake. Can we carry many homes in the world? Can we wend our way between them? Of course we can; this is what we do to survive as immigrants, as people increasingly displaced and re-homed. What has been stolen, taken, abandoned, left behind. The paths cut off and the new ones chosen or forced. The road shows itself to our feet.

I'm turning towards home grateful and ambivalent. Grateful to have a home place in the world that matters so much, and for which I have such deep respect. Ambivalent at the sense of the expected roles closing in around me, their concurrent griefs. The losses of home rising to meet me as I meander back into their space. The air they take from my newly expanded lungs.

Travel as a way of leaving grief for a time, perhaps. Homecoming as a taking up again of the losses that are intrinsically linked to that particular place. Walking as the way of linking the two, home and away, navigating our stories of travel, bearing our new knowledge back into our everyday lives.

6. Yvonne

I love what you say about ceremony. How we fall into routines and break the routines by the space we are in, by the writing, and the surprises of new views after short and long walks. We span the perimeter of Assisi one afternoon and cannot find a familiar path. So there is ritual in our walking, in the quiet rise and fall of our voices and other voices around us. Night coming after a long sunlit day. Ritual of afternoon coffee and evening wine. Taste of tomatoes and basil on our tongues. Laughter buffeted by seriousness offset by silliness. On a fast-downhill walk from Eremo delle Carceri, Francis of Assisi's hermitage, a sudden rainstorm sweeps through the olive groves on the slope ahead and drenches us. We huddle under tall cypresses that line the road, my bright sarong held over our shoulders flapping as the wind whips up. Pilgrims, for sure—to cappuccinos and the laughing eyes of a server in an ambient hillside eatery.

Now, months on, I pull myself back to Assisi with such desire to be there, my breath comes in as a quiet pant, as if I'm walking a low, long Assisi stairway to a narrow alley again. Liminal space. When I am there, I am fully there, walking the narrow paths, our gradually intertwining and unwinding thoughts. Outside of this/that space, I'm pretty certain, everything else is frozen in place and time and will rev back into existence as we begin to leave it again to wend our way home. But I am home. And I'm not. Memory indecipherable from reality at certain moments, the wind and a bird call the same, no matter where my body is. What is home and what is it to walk? Walk as many places as you can. Move your body. It will ease your restlessness that feels, in the warm, sleepless nights, like frustration, but what it is, or could be, is the deep knowledge of your duality—love and family—space and your art, your own body out walking the paths, friend at your side.

7.

What do we find in the dark? Shape-shifting
city, thoughts, desires, selves.

Down back streets, a certain truth:
the soul come home to itself.

Scaffolded. A crane holding
what can be held: limestone bricks, secrets.

What can we hold? A child, a hand.
A shifting powder of time.

Dip a hand to the Piazza fountain. Touch lips.
Touch face. How be a vessel—pouring in, pouring out.

8. Jenna

Months on, and the red fretwork of sun in the topmost
branches of a balsam poplar transports me instantly back to
Assisi. Such an uncanny leap of the mind from the mid-winter prairies to Umbria in the heat of summer leaves my body
momentarily stunned into stillness.

I'm home, but I'm restless, the pinch of winter circumscrib-
ing the days. The brief curve of light before the early darkness.
My body resigns itself to winter walking, the tightened stride
and dropped gravity of a woman accustomed to navigating
on black ice, glare ice—all the different ways my balance can
detonate beneath me. Winter on the prairies leaves my body
aching at the end of the day with the cramped necessity of
holding myself upright. I long for summer's expansive stride
and Assisi's bounded streets, the warmth of the rose stone
walls ensconcing my evening walks with Yvonne.

My mind, too, is constricted: the expected roles of the
teaching term in the city, the genteel boxes of work and home,
social gatherings, meetings. Time is sculpted; it appears lim-
ber, but is not. It's fossilized into routine, and I long for nothing more than to get up and roam, to follow my instinct, to
ramble with my friend. *Why would anyone want to walk out
in this weather?* I am asked time and again. *In this winter city?*
Because walking, finding one's feet, is a way of finding oneself too, of meeting oneself somewhere down the back streets
and endless flights of stairs, just where the arches of the oldest
part of town give way to vistas of the fields. My mind is there
already, spying the Umbrian countryside on the other side of
the wall. My body longs in its bones to follow.

9. Yvonne

Even still . . . months on, the lyrics of *There she goes* . . . linger in my thoughts, especially when I'm out walking, especially if I'm also thinking of you, Jenna, and us on some trail, not paying attention and suddenly, surprisingly, lost.

There she goes . . . vibrates in my head, and I can't help but sing aloud. As Jenna is to flower picking, I am to fragmented notes of song spilling out of me as we walk. I know I drive her nuts, and we two living like a couple as we are these weeks. "There she goes . . ." I sing. "There she goes again . . ." The songwriter, Lee Mavers of the La's, and his band members will not deny that the song is about heroin, but as we walk and wander up and down brick and cobbled streets, I think less of heroin, more the high of women walking, the *flâneuse* exploring the night streets with only a tinge, in this walled village, of what might lurk around the corners and down the ever-narrowing alleys. When we move to Venice, I begin to sing Spirit of the West's "Venice Is Sinking." How time narrows, the past pushing up against the present. Once we are home and fully distracted by daily life, Venice will flood like never before. This is how life runs, in a rising and falling tide of desire and necessity. Change and longing both for the change and for how things are. To be held in the moment—one foot on the rise of a step, lingering note of song, the way sunlight on brick gives the day an orange halo. Laughter and slow, lingering sun that suddenly, in a blink, plops below the horizon, and the walls rise like reaching giants above us.

10. Jenna

I miss the worn hoop of the city walls in Assisi; to a lesser degree, the salt-tinged, over-peopled nights of touristy Venice adrift in its archipelago. I miss the expanded stride of women walking together at dusk through Assisi's pilgrim streets (by choice, after the long heat of the day) and along Venice's canals (by necessity, after the crush of daytime travellers that left the main streets almost impassable). I miss my friend and her constant cheeky songs, her uncanny way of finding exactly the right lyrics for the occasion.

I find the same stride out at my farm after we return to Canada, Yvonne home to the coast, me back to the north country, the Alberta boreal where I live when I'm not teaching. My body remembers the unencumbered walk we learned in Italy, how to move through space as though we owned it, processing our own fear and barriers as we went, noting the looks of others, of men. Safety in numbers, the two of us walking for miles through the Umbrian countryside, treading the evening streets of Assisi that we'd come to know almost by heart. Under the tremendous sky of the August prairie, I walk this way: hips open, pace measured and definite, eyes alight with curiosity. I allow myself to fully own the small space of my body, a coloured woman alone on a tiny township road in rural Alberta. Instead of jasmine, the honey-thick scent of alfalfa in bloom. Instead of swifts, the prehistoric stalk of sandhill cranes, and instead of tourist crowds, the slow trail of an unknown pickup truck behind me as I turn for home at the intersection with the range road.

I try to release the tension in my body as I walk.

I name each fear as it comes.

11.

Return a deep grief,
an acquiescence to walls.

How find this self on the paths
of desire and duty?

How to meet this self in mirrors,
unexpected. How to meet her eyes.

We are full of questions. Hold this—
carved woman, carved dove. Tail of flight.

A spangle of stars, night's dark sweep.
Crescent of moon on the toll bridge home.

12. Yvonne

Months and two seasons after we left Assisi, I walk Mount
Douglas Park with my dog. Usually, we walk early in the
morning, after my son has gone to school and I've worked
for a few hours. Today, meetings and other chaos interrupt,
and though the dog has had a run, I've not had a walk, so off
we go. As I walk, I note the difference of the afternoon light in
this rainforest, compared with morning walks. I talk to you,
Jenna, in my head—I note pools of light on worn bark mulch
paths and leafless cedar branches and wonder what scents
you would grab as your fingers trail over the damp grasses
and barks of these west coast trees. Walking in afternoon's
amber light, I wonder about men who pass, recall an incident a few weeks ago when a man was off-trail and stayed
very still and quiet, then, when I jumped at noticing him, he
said, "I'm so sorry. I didn't want to scare you, so stayed quiet;
I didn't know what to do." Reverse paranoia, I recall, having
recently read about it in an essay by Will Self in a book on
walking.

Despite the amber light on trees, Jenna, I feel safe here
because I've been walking here regularly for years now, steadily for the past year with this energetic dog. Though, as soon
as I think that, then I begin to wonder as a pair of young men
approach. It's fascinating to walk on guard in this way, and

yet to move smoothly between awareness and daydreaming, to ponder Assisi streets and our walk up that epic hill to Eremo delle Carceri, trying out trails that dead-ended, or left us climbing up and over structures. The dog and I decide to go to the top, and so through heavy, fast breaths, I begin to sing the lyrics to a Spirit of the West song—"It's here where I feel it, funny how it's, funny how it's here . . ." the song repeats, those same lines looping around and around in my head. These are my climbing Mount Doug, also called P'kols, lyrics. I will have to sing them to you next time we are walking together.

13. Jenna

Mid-winter, and it's blowing snow and glare ice. The sky is the same colour as the land, an eruption of flakes, and the mercury has just hit minus-30 C. Minus-38, if you count the wind chill, and out on the farm, where we survive on the heat of a wood cookstove, we definitely count the wind chill.

I'm not walking at all, these days; or rather, I spend a great deal of time reliving walks in my memory, and then going out tromping on the snowshoes in my deep winter gear when it's decent outside. Today, the clouds are the dull grey of hammered pewter, the frost is creeping in around the doorknob in spite of the stove's best efforts, and I am going exactly nowhere.

It's easy to revisit Italy in my mind: the simple touch of a button on my phone releases the San Rufino bells in all their clanging, jangling glory. Off-key at the best of times—remember how they reminded us of a bucket band, Yvonne? The same ramshackle assemblage of sound.

In my thoughts, we're climbing the steep stairs, worn smooth by thousands of feet, that rise behind the Piazza del Comune. On our right, a waterfall of jasmine, just past bloom, cascades down over the stonework; on the left, in the window of an abandoned building, a dead pigeon is splayed against the window screen, trapped there from the inside. Every time we climb these steps, we find ourselves pausing under the small shrine of its death, its wing bones slowly bleaching under the July sun.

How is it possible to become so familiar with a place that you can walk it in memory, months later, years? I connect Assisi instantly with a freedom of walking, of your company, my friend, of the ease of women wandering together. The great gift and privilege of it, that sense of ease, and the simultaneous sadness that we *must* feel grateful when we are permitted our own safety. How much I look forward to walking with you again.

14.

The moon changes itself. How to cast
this line of light. Home threading.

Partial eclipse, departure. The way home
not yet defined.

Yes and the bells ring again. Seeking
we find their source—walls lean in.

Find the paths out from under.
On the terrazza, a cloak of sky

and one star. Again, it guides us north.
The path is long. Stepped. Sometimes washed out.

Notes

Brian Brett, "If Doctors Said This Was Your Last Spring, What Would You Do?" *Tyee,* June 20, 2019, www.thetyee.ca.

Will Self, "Is This a Real City," as it appears in *Beneath My Feet: Writers on Walking,* ed. Duncan Minshull (Kendal, UK: Notting Hill Editions, 2018), p. 150.

Lauren Elkin, *Flâneuse: Women Walk the City in Paris, New York, Tokyo, Venice, and London* (London: Chatto & Windus, 2017), p. 26.

Robin Wall Kimmerer, *Braiding Sweetgrass: Indigenous Wisdom, Scientific Knowledge and the Teachings of Plants* (Minneapolis, MN: Milkweed Editions, 2015), p. 37.

FISHING WITH TARDELLI

Neil Besner

I was twelve the first time I went fishing with Tardelli on the *Moby Dick*, twenty-four feet, lapstrake, the used boat my stepfather, Walter ("Unca" in those early years), had bought, he told us the first day we stepped aboard, as a "stepping stone." He was right. His boats got newer, bigger, made to order. His last one, lost on a reef twenty-five years ago, was fifty-two feet.

That Brazilian winter weekday afternoon when I was twelve, I watched Tardelli steal twenty-five litres of gas from another boat by sucking on a thin rubber hose, spitting out the first gout, and siphoning the rest into the *Moby Dick*. Out of sight of the main marina the *Moby Dick* slipped away, clandestine, from the back docks of the Yacht Club with three other sailors—that's what they were called, Brazilians who had washed up into these jobs taking care of these boats—*marinheiros,* mariners—and headed out into the bay. Like almost all the "sailors" at the Club, none of these three could swim. Nor could Tardelli.

When I told Walter (Unca in those years, as I have said) maybe a year later about the gas thefts, he told me I was observing honour among thieves. That sounded fine. At thirteen, fourteen, I was Tardelli's ally, without knowing in which battle, which war, fighting for whom.

Walter is alive in Rio in his late nineties. He has known me since my birth; I have known him since I was six. That, to begin, is how we were. We have not made very much progress since.

I fished with Tardelli in Rio, in and around the bay. We fished for bluefish. We fished with handlines, thick nylon line wrapped around a small board. This type of fishing, called *puxa puxa* in Portuguese (poosha poosha, or pull, pull), has largely vanished now.

Bluefish continue to inhabit every ocean, but in the polluted bay in Rio, they are now much scarcer.

Tardelli died in 1991. I did not go to his funeral; I am not sure that he had one.

Tardelli could not have been more different from my stepfather, his employer for over thirty years. As I knew he would if such a thing were to happen, Walter called me in Winnipeg from Rio to tell me Tardelli had died. In matters such as these Walter has been nothing short of dutiful, predictable. Reasonable.

Thinking of Kafka's "Letter to His Father," a few weeks after Tardelli died I wrote Walter a sorrowing denunciation of six single-spaced pages. I told him that, unlike Tardelli, he was inscrutable; I told him that he was unknowable. I also told him that of course I knew that I would never have met Tardelli, never have come to Brazil, never have lived that fabled life had it not been for him.

Five years later, I made the mistake of giving Walter the letter in Rio. The next day he returned it to me with satisfaction. "You love me," he announced.

To Tardelli's peers he went by his last name; he was one of the few who did not have a nickname. However, the woman who called him to the telephone over the loudspeaker at the Yacht Club always repeated his name once, the second time rising on the last syllable of his first name: *Marinheiro Manuel Tardelli, Marinheiro ManuEL Tardelli*. In memory her voice is measured, warm and singsong, but also officious.

Tardelli calls up no ache, anger, or regret.

I'd always believed that Tardelli's name meant he was, like many Brazilians, of Italian descent, but now I'm not sure. I was never in his small house in Vila Kennedy, a state-sponsored development project named after JFK in the tough west of Rio, now drug battle–scarred, that took him two hours to get to by bus and train from the Yacht Club. I met his stocky wife once when she came from those hours away to bring him something. I met one of his sons, Luis, a bitter young man in his twenties who worked at the Club for a few months and came fishing with us once on my boat. When I asked him—told him?—to move the beat-up wooden fish box, he sneered. *"Sim senhor, o senhor que manda."* Yes, sir, your orders, sir. I got it the second time. Tardelli laughed, face away from me.

Tardelli spoke no English save to mock me or, when we were alone, my stepfather now and again. I taught him *seagull.* "Sai gol," he laughed. I taught him *fish.* "Feesh." He told me that when my stepfather got angry, the back of his neck became a *pescoço vermelho,* turned red. He told me that my stepfather had *um medo filha da puta de morrer,* a son-of-a-bitch fear of dying. When we were out on weekdays fishing alone, he mimicked my stepfather on the days when he'd ask Tardelli to take us back to the Yacht Club for no apparent reason: *"Não bom, Manoel, Iate Clube, Iate Clube,"* no good, Manuel, exaggerating his employer's stilted Portuguese.

Tardelli was never in an airport, never got on an airplane. He disbelieved in flight. In late August each time we said goodbye for the year, he would blow into the palm of his hand: *"Vai te, filha da puta"*—Go, you son of a bitch—laughing. He insisted that I do a proper job of wrapping the fish in newspaper bound with fishing line to take home in the evening; he insisted that I take apart my clumsy scrunch of newspaper and fish and do it again, properly. He mimicked my posture, head down *como uma tartaruga,* like a turtle. One June I found a Christmas postcard in his locker, intended for me but abandoned—the only time I ever saw evidence Tardelli could write. The implications of an address somewhere he barely believed in may have dissuaded him. I was sixteen. Holding the postcard in my hand, I became teary-eyed. I never mentioned this to Tardelli or to anyone else.

Tardelli lusted after and then seduced the cook at home. I never discovered how they'd met. "Speak to me of Floriana," he'd say to me when we were out in the bay. "My cock gets hard just hearing her name." In Portuguese this sounded better. My mother called him Lady Chatterley's Lover, and he was truly handsome. For her and Walter he shaved with soap in his locker, wore carefully pressed whites and clean sneakers. He fished with me in torn shorts, bare-chested and barefoot. I have photos of him in both costumes. They are not contradictory. That would be too simple.

Those Brazilian winters, home as a teenager from boarding school in the US, going fishing with Tardelli in Rio began with lounging carefully along the street near our rented house in Leblon where the cream-and-blue *lotação*, the Urca–Leblon bus, passed. There were no bus stops then and the bus didn't stop fully; you flagged it down and swung on with just the right admixture of casual authority.

The driver shifted gears with dramatic sweeps of the arm. His little fingernail was sharpened and polished. He banged the bus down the street and I dreamed out the window for forty minutes until we got to Botafogo. I swung off the bus and landed on my feet as per unspoken rules. I was fourteen.

I found Tardelli and Elias, Senhor Elias Abreu, or Marili, from the Amazon, sitting in the sun on the small step outside Tardelli's locker, eating rice and beans and a hard-boiled egg out of tin boxes. We had a cigarette. I was learning to flick the ash as Tardelli did from the unfiltered Continentals he smoked, a finger brushing ash from the tip. He walked to the edge of the dock and looked down.

"Clear and cold. No good." Cold water meant bad fishing.

"Let's have coffee first, then we'll go," Elias said, and on our way to the sailors' bar we met Poporoca from Portugal, who slapped me on the back and got his pail with his lines in it and his hooks hanging around the edges and his sack and knife. We met him down at the bar and sat inside on the marble benches and drank strong black coffee and ate a buttered roll. Tardelli went to the water cooler for a long drink, and we walked by Cabo Verde in the fish shop and promised him we'd bring him something.

It was close to three. The *Moby Dick* was ready down at the hangars, out of sight. The wind came from the east, the boats anchored outside the marina pointed their prows in at Urca mountain with Sugar Loaf beside it. We idled out whistling the seagull sound, which meant *"ta grosso,"* it's thick, the fish were there. The empty fish box was streaked with dried blood and chippy with dried scales and the white paste that the fish vomited when they were full of minnows.

When we left to fish on those salty mid-sixties afternoons, sun mid-sky and a gentle wind from the east, Tardelli, mock ceremonial, mock reverential, would slow down to acknowledge the small statue of São Pedro, patron saint of fishermen, on our way out and again on the way back in the gathering dusk. *"Obrigado, São Pedro,"* he murmured, crossing himself.

São Pedro then as now stands on a small reef. He has always lost the upper half of his raised right arm. São Pedro was clothed then in rusting green. Now the state has gilded him in cheap gold. Tardelli was never Catholic, never religious, always spiritual. The slim white herons that now perch on São Pedro's head wouldn't have dared when he was more properly clothed and rusting.

We waved to the women sitting cross-legged on the stone wall over the rocks as we picked up speed again and moved past Urca and the old man anchored at the point. He was there every good day. We came to the entrance of the bay with our lines stretched out behind us to loosen them, and the ocean opened wide in front of us. The east wind sent small white-caps in and the little white gulls with red beaks that cried like lost children were dancing over a stretch of water between the Fort of São João in the middle of the entrance and the Fort of Santa Cruz on the north side. Early one morning Tardelli and I caught ten big bluefish there.

We headed out to the Fort of Imbui with its long, low, white clapboard houses on the beach and its big guns on the cliff, and the islet offshore where the bluefish sulked in the coffee-coloured water.

Poporoca sat on the deck seamy-faced, with one gold tooth. His dirty blue shirt was open at the chest and his cap was pulled down hard against the wind. He sharpened a hook and looked up at us with the sprig of green that he always carried tucked behind one ear, and told us, "Of the three of you, I'll fuck two."

Tardelli laughed. "Of the three I'll fuck three." Elias looked at me. "The old ones are talking again. Of the two of them I'll fuck two." Then he showed me the callused open palm of his hand and crushed out his cigarette on it. "For luck."

Tardelli started to sing one of his arias, and we turned it into "Cielito Lindo" and repeated the "*ai, ai, ai ai.*" Poporoca shook his head at us.

The sun was still high in the sky over Sugar Loaf, but it was starting to go light red as the afternoon took away the noon-day glare and the water began to go calm as the wind died down. It would stop for a moment at dusk and then breeze from the southwest for a time before it turned north for the night. All night the wind came from the north and chilled the lovers on the beaches and then freshened the morning and made the sailboats turn their gull prows out to the Fort. The next day we'd watch the wind. If it didn't circle to the east by mid-afternoon, it was likely to go straight southwest and bring cold and rain and raise up the waves. If it blew for too long, the bay got rough and the cargo ships went horsing out to sea. You couldn't hide from the wind except behind Cutunduba Island, where there were seldom any fish, although one day our boat caught 147 there, and Tardelli stopped after ten fish because he was sick.

We slowed down and idled in close to the rock at Imbui, on the southwestern point, where sometimes there were groupers, and we lay there and waited to see if the soldiers from the Fort would fire shots in the air and wave us away. We watched how the boat rode the current and looked at the colour of the water and felt the strength of the tide. Tardelli put his lure down, took it out, and held it against his cheek to see how cold it was at the bottom.

We watched for the dolphins that came and rode herd on the fish and cut them to pieces. We looked for shark fins and rays. When the rays jumped, it meant the water was cold and the fishing was bad. One winter, the bay was cold for a long time and we came back with five, six fish a day, sometimes none at all. That winter the rays jumped a lot, making tremendous splashes with their wings as they came down. You could see the tumult in the ocean from far off. One ray sunned itself just off the point of the Fort of São João on the protected side, with the tips of its two wings cutting through the water at least six feet apart so that at first it looked like two sharks, until the great flattened-oval mouth came into view and it swirled away from the boat.

That cold winter, Tardelli caught two or three big groupers. To catch a grouper the way we fished was to be lucky. They're bottom fish, and so it was a question of the lure falling right next to the mouth and the grouper being hungry. It felt like a bottom snag at first. Then the line began to come up, very slowly, stretched down against the side of the boat. The grouper continued to pull straight down until it came close to the surface, where it tried to swim away. One afternoon at Imbui, Tardelli caught one of seven or eight kilos, a map of yellow and white and brown, large mouth agog, gills working slowly and steadily in the box. Another boat came alongside and bought it. When we came back that evening, the grouper was lying on the dock, still alive, and the man who had bought it was looking down at it, explaining how hard he had fought it.

Tardelli scowled at his line stretching out quickly. It popped and throbbed between his fists. He looked at us. "It's because I was thinking about Floriana."

Elias laughed at him. "What about the money she wanted for the dentist?" The money, Tardelli told her, it was his greatest wish to give her, she'd come to the right man. "She spoke about money, and it ruined everything. I told her that if she needed money, I was the one, I was the man, and that was it. My cock collapsed when it heard 'money.'"

Sometimes the water went light green and the sun picked out sparkling crystal points in the waves. The bluefish lay at the bottom grim and tight-mouthed. That water could bear little but its own absent dance of bright gilt and green. The sky was far up, too blue, empty. Time stopped the sun and the wind came blind and impersonal. We trolled out in the open, lines trailing. Nothing.

Cargo ships drifted in and out of the bay at a distance. We saw a submarine and joked about the Brazilian navy. Straight north, marking the northeastern limit of the outer bay, lay Father Island and Mother Island, with Island of the Son sheltered between. Father Island is largely bare rock, a few scattered palms clinging to its slopes and a small reef jutting out from the northeast point. When the ocean was quiet, the waves washed low around the rocks, green and white and faintly foam-struck. When it got rougher, we looked from Imbui and the southwest point whitened and then vanished and the ocean in between looked rumpled. It was hard then to judge distance, and the salt smell was stronger and heavier. The boat yawed. The black vultures, the *urubus* that lived on all the islands, soared high, long, and lazy above the palms.

The southwest wind came from behind the mountains that ranged the coast and greyed the sky and massed the clouds heavy with rain and swung the boats in towards the beach at Botafogo, silent white forms on the water, like resting gulls. From the dock we watched the palm trees on the lower edge of Sugar Loaf. If they were bending into the mountain's face and the fronds were shaking, we knew not to go, because outside the wind would be eating the waves. The old trawlers would all be riding at anchor inside the entrance to the bay, and the Fort of São João would be washed over with dull white waves slamming across its rock form, long, cold slaps of iron driving themselves over the Fort to stream back down, ocean that took colours away from their names and buried the dye deep in herself.

The morning was half-gone. Tardelli and I were trolling up and down at Father Island on the southeast point where the sharks were. We were watching a canoe with an old man in it. We saw him tense up and begin to give out line. Then the canoe started to move as the fish carried him. We circled around him, keeping our distance and looking away because the canoe people thought we put evil eyes on them and they swore at us. We wheeled around to keep the canoe in sight as he brought the fish up, hanging half in and half out along the side of the canoe, and we heard the repeating flat thump of the club as he killed the shark, still hanging over the side. He took a long drink from his water bottle and sat, slumped. Weeks later another large shark glided by us there, back fin slicing just a few feet from where we stood. Tardelli swore at it, threw his lure at it.

Once, we saw a lost penguin at the mouth of the bay, come up from far south. It dove every time we came near until Marili grabbed it and put it in a sack. *"Este é o pinguin? Bom dia, senhor pinguin!"* This is a penguin? Good morning, Mr. Penguin! It scrabbled furiously in the sack. We let it go.

I went to Father Island alone once in the small boat and found the fish hungry off one point and caught twelve. I got too excited and threw the matchbox into the water, holding the match in my hand after lighting a cigarette. Like Tardelli one morning at the Fort of Santa Cruz, when I had caught eleven fish and he got flustered changing lures and threw the new one into the water without tying it on.

Memories branching endlessly, but no tree. Wallace Stevens: *There is no wing like meaning.* Or memory as lightning, a scimitar flash.

We reminded Tardelli of his throwing the new lure away at Santa Cruz on the days when it was too rough or rainy to go out and we sat inside his locker and poured heated lead into the wooden mould that one of the carpenters had made for us. We placed a length of wire in the mould, doubled on itself to form an eye at each end. The lead cooled around the wire in the long bullet shape of the lure. We trimmed the edges while the lead was still hot. When twenty or thirty were ready, we painted them, blue, yellow, white with blue spots. We crimped a skirt of fine nylon hair, yellow, white, blue, mixed, to the bottom of the lure with fine wire and a hook was clamped in the eye so that the hair hung around it. The different colours had their names—the clown, the killer. We hung them around the pail with the store-bought lures.

The biggest bluefish I ever saw came on a hot Saturday afternoon at Imbui. Tardelli and I were waiting for the tide, and the fish came alive. We had caught seven or eight when Tardelli swore.

"I've caught bottom." He began to wrap his line back onto the board so that he could hold that and not cut his fingers. He braced himself against the side of the boat and held the board out over the water. Then the line began to give a little and he threw down the board when he had enough slack and pulled the line up slowly. We thought it was a big grouper. Then a large blue-white shape swam broadside into view, the lure—a silver zigzag—trailing from one side of the huge open mouth, teeth showing, and Tardelli whispered, "She's the queen of them all," and slowly lifted her out and draped her in the box. Her tail and more hung over one side, her body beaded with drops of water.

Tardelli struck another big fish like the queen at Imbui a few weeks later that summer and fought with it for a long time. When he brought it in close and leaned down slowly to take the lure in one hand, the fish lifted its head out and shook it, looking at us, gills flared red and wide, and the line broke at the knot and the fish turned over and slowly swam down and away.

The first afternoon I went out, the *Moby Dick* with her high freeboard pitched ungainly over the long afternoon swells. We went out to the green buoy that marked where the *Magdalena* lay, a cargo ship that ran aground on a reef and then sank in the middle of the bay some years earlier, maybe thirty years. The story we heard was that she was carrying a cargo of sugar.

The green buoy sang and moaned in the wind. There was a slow whirlpool directly above the sunken ship, coloured differently from the water at its edges. The ship's masts rose high off the bottom so that you could get snagged among them halfway up your retrieve and think you had a big fish on. The line stretched tighter until it began to sing and then it snapped as the boat rode with the current, and you cursed and said, "I was just stretching the line." Some late afternoons there would be ten, fifteen fugitive boats from the Club, and the canoe fishermen, all making their passes with the tide over the dead ship, coming around again when they'd drifted too far off, everyone watching the others for signs of fish.

On the way back that first time the waves rose blue-black behind us and ran under the stern. I went down to put on my socks and shoes. Poporoca came in and asked if I was afraid. I was. I said no. The waves rose high over the stern and the *Moby Dick* performed what they called the *jacaré*, the crocodile, burying her nose in the black water, shuddering up to slide down another crest. When we rounded the point at

São João Fort with the lights from the city shining over the darkening water and sending glimmers of white and yellow across at us, Elias yelled, "Lights, you bastards!" at the trawler anchored just inside the point in the dark so that we almost rammed her. Tardelli laughed. "That's how they die so young."

At the Fort the big brown-and-white gulls were nesting in their holes in the rock. The little white gulls, *Trinta Reis,* thirty pieces of silver, had gone out to the far islands for the night. The bats and the swallows were circling out from their little caves near the water. In the shelter around the point the water was calm and quiet, and the electric sign on the mountain beside us announced the weather for the next day in running red dots: "Unstable, with rain and temperature in decline." The six o'clock news ran across the face of the mountain in bright tracks reflected on the water. The ghost white of the anchored boats came up on us, masts hanging in the sky as we slanted off towards the hangar. We eased in reverse towards the dock, someone at the prow with the anchor, another at the stern to throw a rope up to whoever was waiting for fish. Tardelli reversed the engine in short bursts, cutting off so that we slid to a stop with the anchor holding and the rope knotted around the bollard.

Now the bargaining began, with the "seagulls" all standing around looking at the fish on the dock. Tardelli pretended he didn't see anyone, ambled around the pile, lit a cigarette.

"Poporoca, Senhor Abreu, take your fish." Tardelli said he's not taking any fish today and then they started. "Tardelli, sell me a good fish," said Turk the baker, pedalling up to us with hot bread on his bicycle cart. "Here's our cousin the Turk, what does the Turk want, I know, the Turk wants fish," Tardelli said. The Turk got off his bicycle to look at the fish and gave us fresh rolls. Tardelli gave him a fish when everyone had gone.

Cats slunk through the shadows. Now and then a figure ambled past Tardelli's locker with a wave and the red eye of a cigarette and an airline bag slung over one shoulder.

All of this—the ambling figures in the evening, the Turk on his bicycle cart, the silent cats—occurred and now recurs. The movements unfold decorously in time slowed, then in time slowly flowing. This motion and its progress and regress are like those of the waves on the beach at Ipanema, at Leblon, that I watched unfurling one upon the other when I was in my twenties and thirties and forties and trying to understand time, because I thought then that I could understand time. I thought the waves could teach me. I thought then that if I could understand time, perhaps I could fathom memory. I thought, then, that the variation in the repetition of every wave's unfurling stood for something vital, something unique about time. I thought, then, of Mr. Ramsay in *To the Lighthouse,* who would never arrive at the understanding he was seeking. Now, it is enough to watch the waves furl, unfurl. To contemplate them. To contemplate.

The fish for home were wrapped properly in newspaper. We strolled down the docks in the dark past the sailboats and the pier stretching out grey against the dark, past the Clubhouse where the nursemaids sat watching the members' children, and Elias nudged Tardelli. "Just mention Floriana, it still grows, don't worry," Tardelli murmured. We said good night to Jorge the barber in his shop, soon to die unexpectedly. *"Jorge fechou,"* Tardelli told me, laughing, when I got back the following summer. Jorge closed. Eight or nine years later, *"Poporoca fechou,"* with a warmer laugh. Poporoca used to tell Tardelli that he knew how to fish once, but he forgot. Tardelli laughed.

We left the Yacht Club through the gate for the sailors, and we walked down the street to the short bridge that arched low over another basin, just under the mountain, where the fishermen kept their canoes. We stopped at the little bar there for a coffee, then walked out to wait for our buses, leaning on the seawall. Below us a man sat over a small fire on the rocks with a tin can filled with mussels beside him, holding a handline wrapped around a Coke bottle and watching it disappear into the dark.

Other buses rolled by. The ocean glimmered white against the rocks beneath us. Tardelli told Elias about the man who was run over the day before by the train. Elias asked him if the man was killed; Tardelli said no, he got up and said, "Wow, what a heavy train." "Funny man," Elias said. They swung onto the bus that would take them to the train station.

My smaller Urca–Leblon bus lurched around the corner and I swung on with my package of fish. The woman beside me looked at the tail coming out of the newspaper and then looked at me and smiled. I kept my eyes down. An hour later I jumped off the bus onto Venancio Flores, crossed the canal, and started up my street. The crazy maid who lit candles on the street corner and talked to herself, staring at something, was muttering in the middle of the street.

The gate stood white against the red steps leading up to the house. The fake lantern above the front door was warm and yellow in the night air, which carried the light, sweet smell of the frangipani trees. I went in the back way and hid the fish in the kitchen. My mother could not stand the sight or, worse, the smell of fish; she forbade them in the house. Outside the crickets sang. The street lights warmed the corners, dark in between the crickets.

The crickets paused to listen. American cars sounded American. The lush brown eye of the night earth, the moist leaves—they watched and listened. They heard the hydromatic click and purr of Park, the silence after the engine was shut off and ticked twice. A car door shut, metal on metal. There were measured steps up to the gate and the scratch of a key in the lock. There was the controlled rasp of shoe leather. Walter was home.

I spent my four high school years in Stamford, Connecticut, at a Jewish boarding school. I came home to Brazil each Christmas for two weeks and each summer for three months, June through August. Thirteen, fourteen, fifteen, sixteen, fishing with Tardelli.

At eighteen I had been in LA at university, at USC, for two years. It was 1968. Walter stood with me one night in mid-June, near the old wooden warehouses and whorehouses at the downtown dock in Rio on another eve of departure, in a fine Brazilian winter mist so that I was wearing the navy pea-coat then in style. I had only come to Brazil to sail north on one of his cargo ships. The *Delilah,* 12,800 tons, sister ship of the *Diana,* loomed metallic and dark grey above us. I want to throw my arms around him. My voodoo heart banged in my head, *Please Unca I'm going crazy.*

No words, nor anything else passed between us, and I made it on board.

I said another goodbye to Tardelli a year later, August of 1969, when I was more profoundly lost. I had begun by then to understand these as ritual fading farewells. We stood on the cement dock in the dark at the Yacht Club, outside the hangar, smoking and looking out across the water at the downtown lights in the flickering city. I was flying back to California that night; my brother was returning to the University of Miami. Within a year, both of us would be back in Montreal, refugees.

In an hour, Walter would drive me and my brother to the airport. In the car I would tell him from the back seat that I was thinking of leaving school. There was a pause of one beat. "That's not very smart, is it?" It was one of the few times I had heard an edge in his voice, one of the rare indications that he was subject to irritation.

When my brother and I were seated aboard our flight, I discovered I was crying; my brother asked me why, but I couldn't say. Four months later, he flew to LA to bring me back to Montreal after I drove my car into the desert outside Bar-stow, California, and left it there after speaking with God at night from the top of a low hill I'd scrambled up. A rattlesnake clattered unseen at my feet. Forty years later, when I described that evening, God and what He'd said, the snake, the stars, to a psychologist in Winnipeg, he asked me if I had heard of vision quests. But by then I was thinking of Spinoza. *All things are alive.* I was thinking of Cohen: *God is alive. Magic is afoot.* A Winnipeg friend said to me: *Sometimes the Universe winks at you.*

Like many Brazilian men of his time Tardelli had many women, many children. That night on the dock in 1969 he told me, *"Eu tenho uma porrada deles espalhado por aí,"* I have a bunch of them scattered out there. He was half-proud, half-rueful, all Brazilian. I uttered some querulous complaint. He glanced at me. *"Voce é jovem, tem muito a apreender."* You're young, you have a lot to learn. No one had ever said such a thing to me. I hear him now through a scrim of years that smell of salt water and unfiltered cigarettes.

Marinheiro Manuel Tardelli, Marinheiro ManuEL Tardelli, the woman sings over the loudspeaker.

I've named my boat here in Lake of the Woods, valedictory, after him.

THE ASHES

Mark Kingwell

Baseball is, and now always will be, my mother's ashes.

She died in March of 2019, lonely in a hospital bed in Victoria, British Columbia. Through the previous fall and winter, I had travelled to be with her and my father several times after a stroke rendered her seriously ill. Their shared living room was a place of endless bickering and everyday troubles. Those visits were full of departure lounges, hospital rooms, filling out tax returns, trying to divine scrawled computer passwords, and dealing with my two competing brothers. Those visits had been so dominated by multiple small tasks that I had not allowed time for emotion, except for one moment when she was wheeled out of intensive care looking like she'd been hit by a truck.

The hospital's houseman called me just after 4:00 a.m. Eastern Time on March 7. He was quiet and solicitous, a calming voice from two thousand miles and three time zones away. I sat on the edge of my bed with my head in my hands, the universal human posture of grief and defeat. I had to teach a seminar the next day, which I barely remember, and then drove straight to the airport. The next days and weeks would bring me all the usual things. My brothers and their families were on vacation in Hawaii, my father is sight-impaired and adept at the learned helplessness so frequent in men of his vintage. In his prime he could navigate four-engine naval patrol planes across oceans. Now he could not even tell me where to find my mother's passport so she could be declared legally dead and released from the hospital's morgue.

I was surprised to learn that, despite her fervent Roman Catholicism, my mother had willed that she be cremated. For all the years of my youth I had repeated the words of the Church's Apostles' Creed, which indicated that, among other things, I believed in the resurrection of the soul and the body. I'm a philosopher, not a theologian. Maybe you can resurrect ashes into a complete heaven-sent body? I don't know.

I have no doubts about my mother's soul, but what makes the body part harder is that we chose to scatter those ashes in different places that were meaningful to her. Some went into the ocean water along the harbour walk near my parents' house. After the somewhat surreal scene of having the box of them queried at airport security, I took some to Jackson's Point on Lake Simcoe, north of Toronto, where my parents had met as lovestruck youngsters at a summer camp. My father was then a monk, one of the Christian Brothers who ran the camp employed as lifeguard and swimming instructor. He was tall and good-looking, with a flashing movie-star smile. My mother was a high school girl working in the kitchen. My wife and I sent some of the ashes swirling into the lake water one autumn afternoon with a chunk of *Ecclesiastes* as benediction.

My father left the monastic order—obviously, or you wouldn't be reading this—and when they were married a few months later, glamour shots of their wedding appeared in all the Toronto newspapers. They were indeed a handsome young couple, the world theirs to take. The Royal Canadian Air Force offered him its own kind of glamour, plus the hierarchy and order they both craved. The next quarter century of service took them, and us, to a new base every two or three years, across the country and back.

I loved this transient life, but it offered few of the usual anchors of childhood. Baseball was always one. My father taught me how to fill out a score sheet, explained the frequently Byzantine rules of the game, with their delicate checks and balances, and indulged in the inevitable games of backyard catch. It wasn't until much later that I realized that my mother was a lifelong fan of the game too. She never talked about it much, and didn't like watching it on television. What she loved was going to games, sometimes with her knitting basket, and sipping the first half of a glass of beer before passing it on to my father or, later, my brothers or me. She couldn't stomach warm beer. She liked double plays and triples more than home runs, like any sane fan. But she always laughed when those Glavine–Maddux–McGwire "chicks dig the long ball" ads came on when we were watching TV together.

Again, like many fans, my mother preferred minor-league ball to the increasingly raucous experience of big MLB parks. I took her to a Blue Jays game at the sound-system-pounding concrete cavern then known as the SkyDome, and she hated it. She was used to the bucolic pleasures of Nat Bailey Field, the AA and AAA site tucked away inside a large public park in leafy Vancouver. She and my father also, like hundreds of other west coast Canadian fans, started taking annual trips to Seattle to see Jays games. But she had far more interest in the outlet stores and cheap dining options until the opening of Safeco Field (now T-Mobile, part of the relentless switcheroo corporate branding trend that she hated). The old Kingdome, which was like a peeling, neglected house by the end of its tenure, made her feel woozy. Baseball was for the outdoors, like football, fishing, and picnics. It was a Sabbath, time out of time.

She had very little interest in the baseball literature that I grew to love, from early *Sports Illustrated* yarns scooped from my older brother's room to the books of adolescence and adulthood: Mark Harris's *Bang the Drum Slowly,* Bernard Malamud's *The Natural,* Paul Quarrington's rollicking *Home Game,* and E.R. Greenberg's underrated *The Celebrant.* In a *sui generis* slot, one had John Updike's unimprovable 1960 *New Yorker* essay "Hub Fans Bid Kid Adieu."[1]

"Greatness necessarily attracts debunkers, but in Williams's case the hostility has been systematic and unappeasable," Updike wrote. "His basic offense against the fans has been to wish that they weren't there. Seeking a perfectionist's vacuum, he has quixotically desired to sever the game from the ground of paid spectatorship and publicity that supports it. Hence his refusal to tip his cap to the crowd or turn the other cheek to newsmen."

Six decades have gone by, and Williams's wish is now a reality: Major League Baseball, despite numerous player infections, opened a shortened, fan-free season in late July. The perusing of baseball books rather than game-day programs used to be a winter diversion; lately, it's the closest many of us have been able to get to the field.

The last time my mother visited me in Toronto, before she became too ill to travel much, she stayed with me in an apartment I was renting in a neighbourhood called Seaton Village. It is a typical chunk of the city's downtown architectural vernacular, with rows of narrow two-storey residential buildings, most semidetached. The place had little sidewalk-bound parkettes, community hockey rinks, and those corner stores that sell everything from milk, ice cream, and potato chips to surprising arrays of hardware, exotic condiments, Korean dumplings, Jamaican beef patties, or Portuguese beef sandwiches.

This area was part of my mother's life tapestry. She went to high school six blocks away from my apartment and lived in a small workingman's house one subway stop farther west. In between, on a route she walked every day from home to school, there is an odd sunken park, a former gravel quarry, called Christie Pits.

The Pits have a multi-layered baseball resonance. In mid-August 1933, five years before my mother was born at a nearby hospital, a six-hour riot broke out in and around Christie Pits in the aftermath of a bitterly contested baseball game. This was in what was then called Willowvale Park—Christie Pits being then considered a little too coarse, though entirely accurate. On one side was the Harbord Playground baseball squad. It was composed mainly of Italian and Jewish boys from the surrounding blue-collar neighbourhoods, populated to this day by families whose first forebears arrived in Canada during successive immigration waves before and after the First World War. The St. Peter's Club nine, opposite them on the diamond that summer, was sponsored by a Catholic church that still stands about four blocks from my old Seaton Village apartment. Both were local teams, but St. Peter's was Anglo Catholic rather than Italian Catholic—or, perceived to be worse, European Jewish.

Ethnic and political tensions were already high in the city. Adolf Hitler had seized power in Germany just six months before, and Toronto's economic fault lines were being ruthlessly exposed during the straitened Depression-era conditions. When a flag bearing a swastika was raised in the crowd during the first of two quarter-final games at Christie Pits, there were angry boos answered by shouts of "Heil Hitler." Two nights later, just as the final out was recorded, a swastika symbol was again displayed, on a blanket this time, and the inevitable fight was unleashed.

The punching and kicking started on the diamond, then spread in increasingly violent running skirmishes involving some ten thousand local residents who had gathered to watch the violence. No one was killed, but dozens were hurt and hospitalized. This small fracas was not even close to the Haymarket Affair, still less to widespread, coordinated atrocities like *Kristallnacht*, but it was still hard to reconcile with

Toronto's projected image of easygoing—if not self-satisfied—diversity and civility.[2]

Christie Pits has been peaceful for many decades since, of course, to the point where it is almost impossible to imagine a half day of *mêlée,* involving thousands of citizens, anywhere near it. This is a quiet, if not quite bucolic, corner of the city's downtown. The primitive landscaping of the Pits park itself features long, sloping concrete walkways at opposite corners—ramps to the little collection of amenities below. There, below street level, you can find a small wading pool, a soccer field, a public pool, and, in the northeast corner of the expanse, a gravel-covered baseball diamond. You can't call it a *park,* really, though the outfield is grass and there is a short cyclone fence there to make home runs real.

The backstop and dugouts are steel tubing and chain-link metal mesh. Behind each foul line is a sad three-tiered bleacher with backless bench seats for about ten people. When games are played here, most fans sit on the sloping grass hillsides. Choice vantages are the very top of the incline where the ground is level, and a little flat hump of land on the first-base side where early birds set up aluminum lawn chairs on the almost flat miniature plateau. A Mr. Softee truck comes to every game, and there is a little concession stand behind centre field where you can buy popcorn and soft drinks.

The whole set-up is more reminiscent of *The Bad News Bears* than of even the most basic Cape Cod, A-Ball, or college field. I recall going to a graduation ceremony at Bard College in upstate New York, and that school, though not exactly a Division-One powerhouse, had a baseball stadium that made Christie Pits look like a sandlot. Thousands of American high schools have better set-ups. But on summer Sundays at 2 p.m., the hometown Toronto Maple Leafs—not to be confused with the hockey team of the same name—dug into the gravel against opponents in the Ontario Intercounty Baseball League: the Barrie Baycats, the Guelph Royals, the Welland

Jackfish, and several others all within a short bus ride from the city. This is semipro ball—a few amateur players just possibly on their way up, some former pros definitely on their way down, and a bunch of just-there players of a talent level well above average but not great enough to make it anywhere else.

It is pretty good baseball; but, more to the point, it is excellent entertainment. The Vancouver Canadians, who play in that beautiful garden park I mentioned before, Nat Bailey (named after the first successful drive-in restaurateur in Canada), are currently the only MLB-affiliated minor-league team in Canada. Once Triple A, they are, as of this writing, Class A Short Season. Other teams in various towns and cities across the country belong to independent leagues, collegiate leagues, or semipro outfits. In Toronto, the closest MLB-affiliated team is the Buffalo Bisons on the other side of the usually busy, now closed Niagara Falls border. So the baseball choices in my town tip precipitously from the double World Champion MLB Big Show Blue Jays right down to this po-dunk neighbourhood park with no seats, no admission fees, and a harried owner who runs up the hill to retrieve any foul ball sent into the gathered few.

My mother loved this place. Once she and my father moved out to Vancouver Island, she only returned to Toronto a few times: a high school reunion, the funeral of a friend, a serious tax issue. Each time, if we could arrange it, we would head over to the Pits on the Sunday afternoon and sit on the hill, letting the familiar rhythms of ball and strike, out and inning, pass the time for us. I would get us Popsicles from the nearby corner store. There was no beer, warm or cold, but there was always Coke or coffee.

My mother was someone often described as difficult, or judgmental, or strict. She was all of these things, not least, I think, because she had to raise three bumptious sons pretty much single-handed while my fly-boy father winged his way from the Azores to the Arctic. She was also loving, loyal, and often sad. Baseball brought her peace. Those infrequent after-noons at Christie Pits were rare times we spent alone together, and I never saw her as happy anywhere else.

When I got back to Toronto, ashes in my carry-on bag, I made a couple of resolves. The scattering on Lake Simcoe was one. The other was this: on Opening Day of the 2020 base-ball season—when, as we all know, time begins—I would take the subway over to Christie Pits and surreptitiously scatter a couple of handfuls in the diamond gravel there. This is a mis-demeanour in my city, I knew, but I was prepared to take the rap if anyone cared to notice.

But then the times changed. Opening Day never came. Our subway system became a petri dish of potential virus contact. The Intercounty League postponed its summer season. Baseball was gone from us, except in forms I found depressing: fantasy games run by a newspaper, pitting dif-ferent eras of Blue Jays against each other, or sports chan-nels reliving glory days by offering "Rewind" broadcasts of memorable games. But the games are memorable because we remember them. For me, as I imagine for many others, a large part of the appeal of sports is watching them in the moment, knowing there is no script and a result that has yet to be deter-mined. Highlights are great, but baseball in particular is about the lived experience of the contest, the way time really does change when there is no clock, and when your biggest deci-sion as a fan might be whether to have another hot dog or a second beer.

What I miss about baseball is of course everything. But what I miss above all is the time spent together with other fans, friends and strangers alike, sharing something so simple that it is surpassingly beautiful, sublime, irreplaceable. I can't get my mother back, and I can't ever watch another game with her. As I write this, it is not clear when anyone will be able to watch a game together with other devotees of the game, in the great democratic proximity of ballparks everywhere. But those memories of Sunday afternoons at the Pits, watching the players scratch out their small paycheques because they just loved to play the game, paycheques you knew would not cover their bills, created that mysterious combination of the ordinary and the elevated that has no name other than magic.

It is a cliché in the baseball world to say, after a failure, *Wait till next year*. (There are at least two baseball books of that title that I know, probably more.) Of course, if I wanted to, I could even now take the long walk to Christie Pits, from my new home on the other side of town, observing correct social distancing along the way, and scatter the ashes. But I choose to wait until next year, when we all hope that baseball will grace our summertime again. Meanwhile, the little box is next to me as I write this.

And I think I'll keep some of them with me forever. Cricket fans know that the idiosyncratic trophy for Test contests between England and Australia is an urn of ashes, allegedly of a burned wicket bail. The origin story is complicated. When the Australia eleven bested the England side in an 1882 contest at the Oval in London, the *Sporting Times* newspaper printed a sardonic obituary for all of English cricket, noting that "the body will be cremated and the ashes sent to Australia."[3] When England travelled to Australia in a quest to regain the notional ashes the next year and prevailed, a group of Melbourne women presented English captain Ivo Bligh with the urn. Bligh later married one of them, the euphoniously named Florence Morphy.

The Ashes are quintessentially cricket, but they also endured because they are a potent symbol of friendly contests, victory and defeat, and the good-humoured year-after-year wonder of sports. Baseball has been taken from us in this plague year, but its remains are safe and cherished. That is what the game means to me, today and forever. The game, and its fans, will eventually be resurrected—in body as well as soul.

The flesh is weak, after all. It craves a cold beer now and then, and maybe that proverbial ballpark hot dog that Humphrey Bogart considered better than roast beef at the Ritz. Any heaven without those plain, exquisite pleasures isn't for me—or my mother.

Notes

1 John Updike, "Hub Fans Bid Kid Adieu," *New Yorker,* October 22, 1960.

2 For documentation of these details, see Daniel Butoni, "Remembering Toronto's Christie Pits Riot," *Globe and Mail,* August 9, 2013.

3 As documented in "The Ashes History, in Pictures: Unforgettable Images from Cricket's Oldest Rivalry," *Telegraph*.co.uk, November 23, 2017.

TO CORONAVIRUS, C
An Anthropological Abecedary
Hilary Morgan V. Leathem

After Paul Muldoon and Raymond Williams

A, Archaeology—Archaeology is the study of the past and its
adherents are archaeologists, who would rather die than be
compared to their popular counterparts like Indiana Jones or
Lara Croft. Archaeologists are curious beasts. Excavations are
marked not only by scientific rituals, like mapping and licking
stones to see if they are bones, but by traditional mating rituals that feature alcohol, meat, and sex. Their informants are
primarily the dead, alongside rocks, pots, and architecture,
which allows them to amass pools of empirical data designed
to re-create life in the past. Their preoccupation with the dead
and predilection for figurative resurrection means they're
astoundingly well equipped for understanding the spread of
viruses, how contagion works, and the physical or sensuous
traces viruses (non-humans, if you will) leave on our bones.
There is an entire field within archaeology focused on societal
collapse. Archaeology already knows what lies ahead for (and
with) the Coronavirus.

B, Black Death—The Black Death occurred in the fourteenth century and was spread by the fleas riding the bodies of rodents. It is credited with completely rewriting Western civilization, probably because it killed off most of the population, allowing for change in a way that basic strikes and shifts to legislation could never deliver. Before the Black Death, people slaved away under the feudal system, which extracted as much labour as possible for no remuneration save for a place to stay (sometimes!). Sound familiar? After the Black Death, because labour became scarce, workers were able to fight for better compensation and rights.

C, Capitalism—If one imagines a god to be something we serve and dedicate our finite energies to, then capitalism is contemporary society's god. Pundits might expound the glory of this system, but capitalism is a so-called "modern" reconfiguration of slavery or feudal practices, predicated on the extraction of labour to create commodities of value. Capitalism depends on a constant surplus of value, conceived of as infinite. The problem? Resources—and human lives and bodies—are anything but infinite. Some anthropologists say we live in an epoch called the Capitalocene, arguing the defining feature of humans today is our obsession with commodities. America is capitalist. Europe is primarily socialist. Coronavirus loves capitalism. Coronavirus was made possible by capitalism and will continue to spread because of capitalism's conditions. Capitalism is not a defining feature of **Civilization**; rather, the mark of a coherent society is, as Margaret Mead once said, care. P.S. Read Karl Marx.

D, Double-Bind Theory—The theory of the double bind, first described by the anthropologist Gregory Bateson, describes a situation where individuals or groups receive conflicting messages that negate one another. At issue is not simply communication, but logic. The double bind can plague groups across society when they are presented with two conflicting demands that initially seem paradoxical, but when unravelled manifest as two distinct logical propositions that are irreconcilable. This causes distress. The Coronavirus creates a double bind for health care workers. If health care workers want to save lives, they must stay clear of Coronavirus, yet they must be around the Coronavirus in order to save the lives.

E, Ecology—The most concise way of understanding ecology would be to point out its etymological roots, which come from the Greek for habitation, *oikos*. Ecological anthropology is the study of how humans adapt to and shape our myriad environments and, in turn, how these unique environments produce differences in our political, social, and economic lifeways. Our environments and landscapes once determined what foods we ate, and even influenced the development of particular architectural styles. Ecology in the time of Coronavirus asks us to consider how the virus will reshape us and our surroundings; we already are seeing how Coronavirus utterly changes our forms of sociality and everyday rituals. Will we alter or extinguish the Coronavirus? **Enchantment** and magic appear at this juncture. To quote from Max Gluckman's 1954 BBC Radio address entitled *The Magic of Despair:* "New situations demand new magic."

F, Functionalism—Functionalism compares society to a living organism; it imagines society as constituted of different parts that must function correctly in order for it to survive. Each part of society, or the "living organism," is a social institution, such as religion, economy, or law. These social institutions developed over time to keep society functioning. So, too, do social institutions have their own distinct function, meaning they fulfill physiological and psychological needs, and are governed by their own set of norms and technologies. Though functionalism is now considered outmoded in anthropology, its primary proponents, Bronisław Malinowski and A.R. Radcliffe-Brown, were highly influential and their ideas echo today. The Coronavirus is an invader disrupting society. Our social institutions, such as science, medicine, and law, are designed to remedy the situation and restore function. But therein also lies the potential for alternative approaches, through institutions like religion or magic, which might explain the "function" of the virus as a supernatural event. Functionalism, when taken to extreme ends, can fuel conspiracy theories.

G, Government—Government is a hallmark of civilization designed to wield power and create order from chaos by imposing the rule of law. As a social institution, it is given to many shapes or systems. We know of democracy, oligarchy, monarchy, fascism, or tyranny. Dictatorships, undesired monarchs in a way, count here, too. The last two centuries have witnessed the rise and fall of all these systems of government. Governments can be good—they can save and protect human lives; governments can be bad—they can enact genocide and wipe out great swaths of their citizens based on their race, ethnic identity, language, class, sexual orientation, religion, and more. With government comes governance, the act of governing—or its failure. Coronavirus challenges governments everywhere and exposes the cracks in our legal foundations. The failure to act in the face of the pandemic is a failure of government, which signifies what, exactly? If government truly is a hallmark of civilization, then does its collapse foretell our downfall?

H, Heritage—Heritage is a paradoxical inheritance. The word's contemporary usage is inextricably entwined with the singular vision of UNESCO's World Heritage list of properties. Heritage can be material—our monuments, landscapes, architecture, antiquities, and heirlooms—or it can be immaterial—cuisine, language, or oral literature. Many people argue that the most powerful form of heritage is the monumental: the grandiose ruins of palaces or temples, from Greece and Egypt to Mexico, Peru, or Zimbabwe. Embodiments of **History** or proof of the passage of time, heritage is also emotional, symbolic, and moral, as the archaeologist Lynn Meskell writes (2015). This is evidenced by the ways that these sites, as well as the immaterial forms of heritage, mediate human relations. Heritage is genealogy, and not only about property but possession. Coronavirus is the universe's response to the question that has plagued heritage studies for the last several decades: To whom does heritage belong? Coronavirus is true universal heritage; it does not discriminate and infects bodies regardless of background. Viruses are communal and collective property; it will own everyone and we will own it. Future humans will look back to the virus as their irrefutable shared past.

I, Immunity—**Ideology**, a system of ideas (and ideals) that shapes our legal, political, and economic worlds (among others), fits here, but **Immunity** is more poignant. Political leaders and scientists throw the word around often, and Boris Johnson and the Tory party touted the notion of herd immunity as one approach or solution to the Coronavirus. The concept of immunity—or being immune—is used not only in science, where it simply means one can no longer contract the virus, but also in the legal sphere, where immunity equates to freedom from liability. In other words, the individual cannot be prosecuted. Immunity emerges as something that is at once empirical and grounded, but also moral. This also extends to sovereign immunity, wherein the government cannot be convicted of committing any wrongs. Coronavirus is not only about a scientific struggle for immunity, but it is a polarizing figure that galvanizes us to scrutinize our governments and those in power—did they commit rights or wrongs?

J, Jingoism—Even before the advent of the Coronavirus, the United States and United Kingdom were practising jingoism, "belligerent nationalism," to quote from *Encyclopædia Britannica*. Both the US and UK are hotbeds of virtuous and aggressive patriotism, though they tend to take different forms. The attitude of "Britain before all else" underpins the Brexit movement, and resembles, quite insidiously, Trump's "Make America Great Again." Current conservative parties on both sides of the Atlantic gesticulate wildly about the inferiority of those outside their borders. The Coronavirus aggravates jingoistic tendencies, driving wedges between and among communities by weaponizing patriotic statements in such a way as to repress counterpoint and oppress whoever is glossed as different.

K, Kinship—Are there fictive kin? Perhaps not. The old adage goes: "You can choose your friends, but you can't choose your family." Anthropologists once made kinship charts of societies across the globe in order to understand if there was a universal law governing kinship, such as the idea that one must be related by blood. There is none. One creates their own modes of kinship through adoption, for example, or through disowning family members who might be too toxic or abusive. Kinship is a form of social cohesion. Coronavirus stands to utterly reconfigure our notions of kinship through the ways it modifies or severs typical relations. Most citizenship laws are products of nation-states that envisaged nationality and kinship as the same, tied to blood and thus the land. After the virus, we may think of kinship differently.

L, Landscape—Coronavirus alters the landscape: the ways we view it, the ways we relate to it, and the ways we inhabit it. Anthropologists (and archaeologists) of the landscape might look at what it means to dwell, the emotions that different landscapes evoke, and how they are built and utilized. Humans, it is said, transform landscapes and are, in turn, transformed by the landscapes. Lands are natural and cultural assemblages full of multiple meanings. A land might be locally conceived of as happy, blessed, depressed, or haunted. Some say landscapes absorb energy from past events and human activity leaves psychic imprints or wounds in the land. These sedimentations of meaning paint landscapes as dynamic and important focal points of our collective existence. Landscapes in the time of the Coronavirus are suddenly conceived of as either facilitating or inhibiting the virus's flow, as scientists and politicians speculate on whether certain climates or seasons and other natural features render Coronavirus more or less powerful.

M, Mask—Masks emerged as ritual or ceremonial objects. Deeply symbolic, their purposes are myriad and may be used for disguise, transformation into preternatural beings or animals, amusement, or protection. They may even offer avenues into communing with ancestors. Yet rather than donning masks to ward off evil spirits or contact deceased loved ones, our masks protect us from another invisible enemy: the Coronavirus. During previous plagues, doctors wore masks for both literal and figurative protection. Scientists tell us to wear a mask, but the power of masks originates in the rituals that assign them **Magical** efficacy. Rituals, argued the symbolic anthropologist Victor Turner (1967), make the obligatory desirable. While we may find masks aesthetically displeasing, their sudden necessity quickly integrates them into the seams of our social fabric, transforming our world.

N, Nation-State—Amidst the outbreak of Coronavirus, Governor Gavin Newsom declared California a nation-state. On the other side of the Atlantic, Brexit finally crystallized, which may be another re-emergence of the nation-state. What does this mean, and why does it matter? States are geopolitical entities, but nation-states presume that there is a common cultural core. Imagined communities, Benedict Anderson once wrote, nation-states have all the same parts as a simple state but are festooned with extra trimmings that can, in some instances, make for dangerous sentiments, such as bigotry. A common ancestral, ethnic background or shared past and traditions can make societies cohere by instilling pride and belonging. When skewed far to the left or right, however, ethnonationalism takes over. The Coronavirus ignites nationalist sentiments because nation-states imagine themselves as independent yet cohesive socio-political entities; the nation-state protects the communities by defeating what's foreign and invasive, fortifying its mythic borders. Brexit and a sovereign California represent insular fantasies just as much as they provide commentary on the successes and failures of government. Designed to be global players, the nation-state preserves the local.

O, Orientalism—Derived from the Orient, meaning east of the so-called Occident or West, the purported epicentre of civilization, the term is colonial and oppositional, creating difference by imagining the East as the West's **Other.** Orientalism was elaborated by the Palestinian-American scholar Edward W. Said in his book *Orientalism* (1978). One of the foundational texts of post-colonial studies, Said excavated Orientalist fantasies from the eighteenth and nineteenth centuries to highlight the patronizing attitudes inherent in Western representations and imaginings of Arab societies, but the term (and its attitudes) extends beyond this region into East Asia. Considered exotic and backward, these cultures are simultaneously uncivilized and desirable. Trump's gloss of the Coronavirus as the "Chinese Virus" is deeply powerful, resurrecting Orientalist discourses, which re-create and reinforce difference between imagined West and East.

P, Possession—Possession has multiple connotations. It can be socio-economic in its usage, denoting an item that belongs to an individual or a people. Patrimony is both an individual and collective possession, as it refers to inheritance in all its forms. Possession, then, is about property. Yet possession also can be spiritual or religious. Traditionally, an anthropology of possession means dealing with how and why spirits, demons, or other invisible entities come to occupy or possess human bodies. It is also medical. Folk medicine in Mexico, for example, revolves around cases of *espanto* and *susto* ("terror" or "fright"), illnesses caused by being possessed by "bad winds" acquired via deities or witchcraft. A sort of exorcism is performed by a *curandera* as the remedy. The Coronavirus is a harbinger of fear and uncertainty; it possesses our bodies and is a plague of fright that cannot be exorcised in any religious sense. Whether it is a bad wind or not, the virus incites deep fears regarding control and the inhabiting of our own bodies. It begs the existential question: Why this, why now?

Q, Quarantine—A medically enforced isolation that is often imposed on only the infected. The life and path of the Coronavirus makes it unique. Delayed symptoms and easy transmission force the whole of society to shack up indoors. Anthropology is defeated by quarantine because we work with people. What does the anthropology of quarantine look like? Will it be ethnographies of Netflix consumption or investigations into human relations with machines and animals?

R, Race—Race is a social construct, which means exactly what you think—humans create it through social relations. Biological anthropologists have even shown us that more genetic variation exists between members of one group (like Italians or Koreans) than geographically distant groups. Translated: my Croatian grandmother may share more, genetically speaking, with someone in Peru than a neighbour in Dubrovnik. Since race is a social construct, its persistence depends on its belief and performance; part of the reason society sustains race is that it is instrumentalized and weaponized in the name of power. Race plays a pivotal role in pandemics, currently and historically. Coronavirus exposes gaps and cracks in a system purportedly designed to serve everyone equally; America's ever-increasing death toll echoes with the ringing of massive disparity. As Chicago and Detroit reported, nearly 70 percent of all Coronavirus deaths are amongst African-Americans from underserved or working-class communities. This is not at all new. Smallpox and yellow fever are pandemics from previous ages that ravaged Indigenous or non-white populations because of their lack of immunity, reinforcing further racial hierarchy through what some call immuno-privilege. In this instance, the death toll is less about a biological immuno-privilege and more about socio-economics or access to health care.

S, Sex—One of the most recent health crises of the last century was the AIDS pandemic, where sex—and **Sexuality**—took centre stage. Given that HIV, and consequently AIDS, was primarily spread through sexual transmission or other forms of swapping bodily fluids, one of the first concerns regarding "Love in the Time of Coronavirus" was whether sex would be safe—can the virus also be sexually transmitted? The AIDS pandemic was deeply stigmatized not only because of the mechanisms of its transmission, but because of the ways sex, sexuality, gender, race, and class became intertwined to fuel more prejudiced attitudes towards the LGBTQ2SI community. This previous pandemic disproportionately affected gay, Black, working-class men. Coronavirus is working in a similar way. While it may not primarily affect the LGBTQ2SI community, it undoubtedly affects those whom late capitalism does not favour. Furthermore, that this pandemic is one where we are quarantined makes sex one of the few available pleasures. Anthropologists like Margaret Mead recognized the human need for sex and the expression of desire. Sex toy sales are booming, but there is also a dark side:

a rise in domestic abuse and violence. Post-pandemic, rather than a baby boom as some media outlets have predicted, we may see divorce rates skyrocket. In addition, we may also witness the return of past struggles. For example, women and the LGBTQ2SI community might find themselves needing to reassert their rights in both the domestic and public spheres.

T, Taboo—Various news outlets assert that a Chinese man ate a bat, leading to the emergence of the Coronavirus. The sentiment that he should not have eaten the bat forces us to reckon with the notion of taboo. Eating bats is taboo according to Western perspectives, as bat meat (and many other forms of animal flesh) is not consumed. A taboo is relative; it is a socially sanctioned and unspoken rule. Because taboos are designed to protect individuals in a society, violating or flouting a taboo may create fear and lead to punishment. Its etymology comes from Polynesia, though which exact language it's derived from is unknown. *Tabu,* they say, means forbidden or sacred. Classic anthropology says that taboo lends society a sense of order and establishes boundaries between the sacred and the profane. Food is a popular subject of taboo; the anthropologist Mary Douglas wrote *Purity and Danger* (1966), which sought to explain the logic of Old Testament food prohibitions. Taboos, she concluded, operate via a dichotomy of what is pure and what is dirty, the latter being dangerous.

U, Universal—The Coronavirus is a universal; it affects (and infects) everyone. Structuralism, a school of anthropology pioneered by Claude Lévi-Strauss, posited that what British anthropology termed social institutions were cultural universals, cognitive traits like mythology and ritual, that structured societies across the world. Lévi-Strauss was an aid to UNESCO, shaping their cultural policy, and may have introduced the language of (or offered intellectual support for) universal human rights and values. Today political organizations mobilize the language of the universal frequently.

V, Virus—An infection, an invader, or an invisible enemy, formal encyclopedic entries cast the virus as an agent that infects all living organisms, whereas its etymology links it to poison. From a linguistic standpoint, the vocabulary surrounding and defining the word *virus* is alarmist and akin to language taken up during war. In her book *Geontologies* (2016), the theorist and anthropologist Elizabeth Povinelli views the "Virus" as one of three critical figures of what she terms *geontopower*, a form of governance that regulates the distinction made between life and non-life. She links the Virus to collective speculation of the figure of the Terrorist (again, echoes of an unstoppable invader). But most important here is how the Virus, and the Coronavirus specifically, disrupts our previous social arrangements. Viruses exist outside the normal boundaries of what we think of as containing life or being dead. Even before Coronavirus was Trump's "Chinese Virus," it was already a foreign threat. The phrase "going viral" will never be the same.

W, Witchcraft—While the persecution of women that characterizes American witchcraft hysteria is particular, there are cross-cultural ideas of witchcraft that focus on the ways that the witch, who might be male or female, acts as an anti-social being that destroys social relations. Anthropologists are less interested in assessing whether witchcraft and the **Witch** are real, and are more taken with the role or impact of a belief in witchcraft on any society. Witchcraft, according to a classic study by E.E. Evans-Pritchard (who notably saw "witchcraft on its path"), is an innate ability, and its role in society is to offer logical explanations for the misfortune of others. Alongside conspiracy theories, the Coronavirus pandemic will spur new speculations on its magical or human-made emergence as people confuse the borders between science, magic, and religion. The virus is witchcraft.

X, Xenophobia—As several of these entries make clear, one of the consequences of Coronavirus—and indeed what allows it to possess its powerful hold over people, inciting fear and panic—is xenophobia. Fear of the other or fear of the foreign, Coronavirus is unknown and foreign on two counts: it is both a newly identified and transmitted virus and first emerged in China. Pandemics, war, famine, and other traumatic events in history see the twinned phenomena of humans practising either care or violence. Xenophobia is sustained or buttressed by polarizing media, which teach us that, as the "Chinese Virus," we should fear anything associated with Asia.

Y, YouTube—Coronavirus troubles or kills off our daily routines or rituals. It has disrupted our normal modes of socializing, making us more reliant on social media and the digital world as a way of connecting and sustaining our relationships. Yet the problem with platforms like YouTube, Facebook, Twitter, or even Zoom lies in how they are cesspools of false information. Because of the extraordinary coupling of social media's sudden necessary role in our life and its accompanying lack of regulation, lies and "alternative facts" proliferate. Previously spaces for the occasional and playful reimagining of human relations, YouTube, Facebook, Twitter, and other social media platforms become dangerous supplements or, even more, substitutions for actual human face-to-face connection. This is far from better than the real thing.

Z, Zoonotic—Zoonotic diseases are infections transmitted between humans and animals or insects, or, in other words, between humans and non-humans. Most people have heard of Lyme disease and rabies; by contrast, most had not heard of coronaviruses until February. Zoonotic is a musty, limited classification of our world—it entails the construction of a dichotomy that is quite futile. It presumes that categories like nature and culture are neatly bounded, when they are in fact porous, dynamic, and prone to wild confluences. The Coronavirus's sweeping success proves there are no boundaries between humans and non-humans and that these separations are shaped by epistemologies and cosmologies. Archaeology has long recognized humans and non-humans are entangled; anthropology that pursues multispecies research would view zoonotic as a Western artifact. However corny, Earth, humans, polar bears, raccoons, and that mould in your shower are all one.

Bibliography

Douglas, Mary. *Purity and Danger*. London: Routledge, 1966.

Evans-Pritchard, E.E. *Witchcraft, Oracles, and Magic among the Azande*. Oxford: Oxford University Press, 1976.

Gluckman, Max. "The Magic of Despair." In *Order and Rebellion in Tribal Africa: Collected Essays*. New York: Free Press of Glencoe, 1963.

Meskell, Lynn. "Introduction." In *Global Heritage: A Reader*. Hoboken, NJ: Wiley Blackwell, 2015.

Povinelli, Elizabeth. *Geontologies: A Requiem to Late Liberalism*. Durham, NC: Duke University Press, 2016.

Said, Edward W. *Orientalism*. New York: Pantheon Books, 1978.

Turner, Victor. *The Forest of Symbols: Aspects of Ndembu Ritual*. Ithaca, NY: Cornell University Press, 1967.

CONTRIBUTORS'
BIOGRAPHIES

Born in Montreal, **Neil Besner** grew up in Rio de Janeiro. He
has travelled, taught, and lectured widely in Brazil. He taught
Canadian literature at the University of Winnipeg from 1987
until his retirement in 2017. His last administrative post was
as Provost and Vice-President, Academic (2012–17). He writes
mainly on Canadian literature, the short story, and the poet
Elizabeth Bishop, with books on Mavis Gallant (1988) and
Alice Munro (1990), an edited collection on Carol Shields
(1995), and numerous articles and reviews, as well as co-edited
collections of poetry and short stories. He is fluent in Portuguese; his prize-winning translation into English of a Brazilian
biography of Elizabeth Bishop (2002) was a major source for
the 2013 feature film *Reaching for the Moon*. From 2004 to
2020 he was the general editor of the Laurier Poetry Series (LPS), a contemporary Canadian poetry series with Wilfrid
Laurier University Press, with over thirty volumes published
to date. Since 2017 he has lived in Toronto. He continues
to travel frequently to Brazil. An avid fisherman, he spends
four months each spring and summer on Lake of the Woods
in northwestern Ontario. "Fishing with Tardelli" is the first
chapter of a memoir that will be published in Toronto by ECW
Press in spring 2022. At present he is working on a biography,

set in Brazil, of the Brazilian baby born in 1960 and raised by three formidable women in Samambaia, near Petropolis, in the mountains outside Rio: Elizabeth Bishop, American dancer Mary Morse, and Brazilian architect and intellectual Lota de Macedo Soares.

Award-winning poet and memoirist **Yvonne Blomer** is the author of the travel memoir *Sugar Ride: Cycling from Hanoi to Kuala Lumpur* and three books of poetry, most recently *As If a Raven*. Yvonne served as the City of Victoria poet laureate from 2015 to 2018. In 2017, she edited *Refugium: Poems for the Pacific* and in 2020, *Sweet Water: Poems for the Watersheds,* both with Caitlin Press. The anthology *Hologram for PK Page* will be released in 2021 and *The Last Show on Earth* is forthcoming with Caitlin Press in 2022. Yvonne lives, works, and raises her family on the traditional territories of the WSÁNEĆ (Saanich), Lkwungen (Songhees), and Wyomilth (Esquimalt) peoples of the Coast Salish Nation.

Catherine Bush is the author of five novels, including the climate-themed *Blaze Island* (2020), a *Globe and Mail* Best Book and Hamilton Reads 2021 selection. She has written and spoken internationally about addressing the climate crisis in fiction. She lives in Toronto and is an Associate Professor and Coordinator of the Creative Writing MFA at the University of Guelph.

Jenna Butler is an award-winning Canadian poet, essayist, editor, and professor. She is the author of three books of poetry, *Seldom Seen Road, Wells,* and *Aphelion;* two collections of ecological essays, *A Profession of Hope: Farming on the Edge of the Grizzly Trail* and *Revery: A Year of Bees;* and the Arctic travelogue *Magnetic North: Sea Voyage to Svalbard.* She is the editor of more than thirty books of poetry and fiction in Canada and abroad. Butler's research into endangered environments has taken her from America's Deep South to Ireland's Ring of Kerry, and from volcanic Tenerife to the Arctic Circle on board an ice-class tall ship, exploring the ways in which we have an impact on the landscapes we call home. A woman of colour engaged with multi-ethnic narratives of place, Butler teaches creative and environmental writing at Red Deer College in Alberta. She lives and works with the land on an off-grid organic farm in northern Treaty 6, the traditional territories of the Cree, Niitsitapi (Blackfoot), Saulteaux, Nakota Sioux, and Métis.

Elizabeth Dauphinee teaches International Relations at York University in Toronto. She is the author of *The Politics of Exile* (Routledge, 2013) and the founding editor of *Journal of Narrative Politics.* She lives in Barrie, Ontario, with her husband and two sons.

Eva-Lynn Jagoe is the author, most recently, of *Take Her, She's Yours* (Punctum Books, 2020), a memoir that explores psychoanalysis, subjectivity, and gender through an intimate narrative. She is a professor at the University of Toronto, where she teaches cinema, literature, creative writing, and environment in the Spanish Department and in Comparative Literature. Eva-Lynn is also a certified Iyengar yoga instructor, and farms a small homestead in the Kootenays, BC.

Mark Kingwell is a Professor of Philosophy at the University of Toronto, a fellow of the Royal Society of Canada and of the Royal Society of Arts (UK), and a contributing editor of *Harper's Magazine.* He is the author of a number of books, including the linked essay collections *Unruly Voices* (2012) and *Measure Yourself against the Earth* (2015), as well as *Fail Better: Why Baseball Matters* (2017). His most recent works are *Wish I Were Here: Boredom and the Interface* (2019), which won the Erving Goffman Prize in media ecology, *On*

Risk (2020), and *The Ethics of Architecture* (2021). In fall 2021, together with Joshua Glenn and designer/decorator Seth, he helped complete a trilogy of compact glossaries with *The Adventurer's Glossary*. His columns and essays appear in the *Globe and Mail, Maclean's,* the *Literary Review of Canada, Gray's Sporting Journal,* and *Harper's,* among others.

Frances Koziar has had more than eighty pieces of prose and poetry published in over fifty different literary magazines, and is seeking an agent for NA high fantasy novels and diverse children's fairy tales (PBs). Her writing frequently grapples with privilege, trauma, otherness, and loss, and has shortlisted in three North American contests. She spent a year as a microfiction editor at a literary magazine, and has also served as an author panellist at an arts festival and a flash fiction contest judge. She is a young (disabled) retiree and a social justice advocate, and she lives in Kingston, Ontario. Website: franceskoziar.wixsite.com/author

Hilary Morgan V. Leathem is a writer, Rhysling-nominated poet, and anthropologist of heritage. They received their PhD in Anthropology from the University of Chicago in 2021. A former Fulbright-Hays DDRA fellow, Leathem is currently an MA in Poetry candidate at Queen's University Belfast and a Visiting Fellow at Maynooth University. Their essays have appeared in *Geist, Jadaliyya,* and *Folklore Thursday,* while their poetry and translations can be found in *Strange Horizons, Augur Magazine, Bending Genres,* and *Phantom Drift,* among others. Leathem's academic writing appears in the *Archaeological Review from Cambridge, Current Anthropology,* and the *Monument Lab Bulletin.* Find Leathem on Twitter: @hmorganvl"

Stephanie Nolen is the global health reporter for *The New York Times.* She is an eight-time winner of the National Newspaper

Award, and an eight-time winner of the Amnesty International Award for Human Rights Reporting. She has reported from more than 80 countries around the world. She is the author of *28 Stories of AIDS in Africa* and *Promised the Moon: the Untold Story of the First Women in the Space Race*. She lives in Nova Scotia.

Kevin Patterson is a writer and physician. He lives on Salt-spring Island.

Soraya Roberts is a freelance culture writer who has written regularly for *Hazlitt* and the *Walrus* in Canada, as well as publications such as the *New York Times Magazine,* the *Atlantic,* and *Harper's* in the US. She was the culture columnist at *Longreads* until 2020 and is currently editor-at-large at *Pipe Wrench* magazine. She is the author of *In My Humble Opinion: My So-Called Life* (ECW, 2016) and is working on a book about cultural criticism.

Ian Waddell (1942–2021) served in Parliament from 1979 to 1993. He was almost elected Provincial in 1996 and served as Minister of Small Business, Tourism and Culture in 1998, and Minister of Environment, Land and Parks from 2000–2001. He wrote *Take the Torch: A Political Memoir,* among other titles.

Sheila Watt-Cloutier resided in Iqaluit, Nunavut, for fifteen years and now has returned to her hometown of Kuujjuaq, Quebec. From 1995 to 1998, she was Corporate Secretary of Makivik Corporation, and elected President of Inuit Circumpolar Council (ICC) Canada in 1995 and 1998. In 2002, Ms. Watt-Cloutier was elected international Chair of ICC. On behalf of ICC Canada, Ms. Watt-Cloutier received the inaugural Global Environment Award from the World Association of Non-Governmental Organizations in recognition for her POPs work and the 2004 Aboriginal Achievement Award for

Environment. In 2005, she was honoured with the United Nations Champion of the Earth Award and the Sophie Prize in Norway, and was presented with the inaugural Northern Medal by the outgoing Governor General of Canada, Adrienne Clarkson.

Joyce Wayne's essay "All the Kremlin's Men" is about her father, a leading member of the Jewish wing of the Canadian Communist Party during World War II. She is the author of *Last Night of the World,* a spy thriller that focuses on the Canadian-based spies exposed by the Soviet embassy cipher clerk Igor Gouzenko. Freda Linton, an actual agent for the Soviets during the war, is the central character. Wayne worked as an editor at *Quill & Quire* and as the editorial director of non-fiction at McClelland & Stewart Publishers. She taught journalism at Sheridan College, where she launched the Canadian Journalism for Internationally Trained Writers Program for refugee and migrant journalists. Currently, she is writing about the double lives of left-wing activists during the 1960s student protest era. She was born and raised in Windsor, Ontario.

Rob Winger is the author of *It Doesn't Matter What We Meant* and three previous collections of poetry, including *Muybridge's Horse,* a *Globe and Mail* Best Book and CBC Literary Award winner, which was also a finalist for a Governor General's Literary Award, Trillium Book Award for Poetry, and Ottawa Book Award. He lives in the hills northeast of Toronto, where he teaches at Trent University.

NOTABLE ESSAYS OF 2020

Meghan Bell. "Take My Money."
The Walrus 17,1 (January/February 2020)

Tim Bowling. "The Floating Library."
Queen's Quarterly 127,2 (Summer 2020)

Daniela Elza. "But Where Are You Really From?"
Queen's Quarterly 127,4 (Winter 2020)

Ethan Lou. "What a Time to Be in Decline."
Hazlitt (November 20, 2020)

Dimitri Nasrallah. "Dancing Bear."
The Walrus 17,6 (July/August 2020)

Kathy Page. "The Astronaut's Wife, the Cyanide Pill, and the Child behind the Windshield."
The New Quarterly 153 (Winter 2020)

MAGAZINES CONSULTED FOR THE 2021 EDITION

Antigonish Review, Arc Poetry Magazine, Brick, Canada's Hist-ory, Canadian Notes & Queries, Dalhousie Review, [Edit], Event, The Fiddlehead, Filling Station, Geist, Globe and Mail, Grain, Granta, Hazlitt, Literary Review of Canada, Maisonneuve, The Malahat Review, The Nashwaak Review, The New Quarterly, Newfoundland Quarterly, Prairie Fire, Prism International, Queen's Quarterly, Room, University of Toronto Quarterly, The Walrus

ACKNOWLEDGEMENTS

"Anatomy of a Pandemic" by Kevin Patterson first appeared in *The Walrus*. Reprinted by permission of the author.

"Upirngasaq (Arctic Spring)" by Sheila Watt-Cloutier first appeared in *Granta*. Reprinted by permission of the author.

"Tick Tock" by Stephanie Nolen first appeared in *The Walrus*. Reprinted by permission of the author.

"All the Kremlin's Men" by Joyce Wayne first appeared in *Literary Review of Canada*. Reprinted by permission of the author.

"Writing the Real" by Catherine Bush first appeared in *Canadian Notes & Queries*. Reprinted by permission of the author.

"The Meaning of Poor" by Frances Koziar first appeared in *Canadian Notes & Queries*. Reprinted by permission of the author.

"Wonder Women" by Soraya Roberts first appeared in *Hazlitt*. Reprinted by permission of the author.

ACKNOWLEDGEMENTS

"The Finca" by Eva-Lynn Jagoe first appeared in *The New Quarterly*. Reprinted by permission of the author.

"The Medium of the Archive" by Elizabeth Dauphinee first appeared in *The New Quarterly*. Reprinted by permission of the author.

"This Is Not the End of the Story" by Ian Waddell first appeared in *Literary Review of Canada*. Reprinted by permission of the estate.

"The Future Accidental" by Rob Winger first appeared in *Brick*. Reprinted by permission of the author.

"On Leaving and On Going Back: Women Walking" by Jenna Butler and Yvonne Blomer first appeared in *Prairie Fire*. Reprinted by permission of the authors.

"Fishing with Tardelli" by Neil Besner first appeared in *Prairie Fire*. Reprinted by permission of the author.

"The Ashes" by Mark Kingwell first appeared in *Literary Review of Canada*. Reprinted by permission of the author.

"To Coronavirus, C: An Anthropological Abecedary" by Hilary Morgan V. Leathem first appeared in *Geist*. Reprinted by permission of the author.

Bruce Whiteman was a rare book specialist for over thirty years. He worked at McMaster and McGill Universities in Canada, and later ran the William Andrews Clark Memorial Library at UCLA. He is now a poet, translator, and reviewer. He teaches courses in the School of Continuing Studies at the University of Toronto, and for several years was the Poet in Residence at Scattergood Friends School, a Quaker boarding school in Iowa. The final book of his long poem, *The Invisible World Is in Decline*, is forthcoming in 2022.